Voyage to Happiness

A book on how to always be happy!

Sanchita Pandey

First published in 2016.
This edition published in 2020

ISBN-13: 9798639390319

Cover Designed by Sangeet

DEDICATION

I dedicate this book to my dear readers who have joined my quest for learning to lead a happy and fulfilled life. Welcome to this great voyage of self-realization, truth and spiritual awakening. Upheavals or success, sorrow or celebration, YOU — the reader, will live your life in happiness!

VOYAGE TO HAPPINESS
A note from the author

A successful life means a life filled with happiness, love and peace. When you are happy, you attract positive people and circumstances as well as abundance in your life.
James Allen has said, **"Circumstances do not make a man; they reveal him to himself."** The best time to start smiling and spreading happiness is NOW!

Happiness must be a way of life for all of us. We must derive happiness not only from the outside world, our surroundings and material things, but also from fulfilment of our innate desires. The happiness which comes from within you, stays with you perpetually. You always remain energetic and smiling because you fall in love with life itself. You enjoy a passion, a mission in life which elevates your way of thinking. You want to get better and are engaged in the pursuit of improving your vocation.

When you are happy, you spread happiness all around. Thus, a cycle is created and you get back love and a beautiful and peaceful life in return. This sounds so simple and yes, it *is* simple. We compound our lives by comparing ourselves with others, by seeking revenge for their past faults and by worrying about our future. This robs us of our happiness and even if we have the key to happiness within ourselves, we fail to unlock it.

However, this journey — a quest for happiness which we will take together will introduce us to our real being.

v

Let us begin our Voyage now and discover our hidden treasure of happiness!

CONTENTS

Preface   viii

Acknowledgments   x

1 Happiness Begins With You!   1

2 Optimism vs. Pessimism   4

3 Bury the Past   9

4 Fire of Anger   16

5 Freedom from Fear   22

6 Each Day is a Festival   25

7 Positive Self-Affirmation   28

8 Power of Gratitude
   in Your Life   37

9 Substitute Worry with Prayer   44

10 Surrender: This too Shall Pass   47

11 Take to Sports   52

12 Contentment   56

13	Invest in Yourself	62
14	Value Relationships	69
15	Don't Judge Others	85
16	Taking Care of Nutrition	89
17	Listening to Music	94
18	Joy of Giving	99
19	Good Health and Happiness	105
20	Learn from Nature	112
21	What Should You Carry with You?	116
22	No Failure is Final!	121
23	Keep Your Faith in God	125
24	A Happy Life is a Successful Life!	129
25	Journey Within, Journey Without	141
	About the Author	150

PREFACE

What is happiness? Why are we all not always happy? What is required to change us from a person brooding, sad and filled with anguish, to a person who resonates with happiness? Why this feeling of heaviness while travelling the road of life?

One day a well-placed, educated lady asked me this question — "What is needed to be happy?" And lo! my own mind started wondering, not about what would be the answer to this question, but to the fact that this lady had a wonderfully paying job, was a respected individual in society and had a very happy family life.

Then, why did she ask such a question in the first place? What was the shift of attitude required to make her feel happy? **One thing was clear: all your material gains could bring you comfort but not necessarily happiness.** However, this question set the ball rolling for many discussions, voracious reading and thinking.

Let us start from the very beginning: Happiness is actually a state of mind and is our own inherent nature. It lies within each one of us and still, in our ignorance, we try to find it in various sources outside. Although we are successful in deriving happiness from our achievements or material belongings, this happiness is transitory. It is not of a permanent nature and so in no time, we find ourselves lost in our day-to-day activities, go through the daily grind of work but at the end of the day, feel stressed and tired.

This book will be your guide in your journey to live a happy life. *Always remaining happy will become a way of life for you, not only in your daily life, but also when you experience tough times in your life!* The only requirement is to be like an empty cup in which new ways of thinking and new beliefs can be poured into.

Certain spiritual aspects will also be discussed which are useful in practical life. They have actually been applied and experimented by me and have borne positive results! A few changes in our way of thinking can help us find this diamond within and travel through life light and happy. That means a **JOLLY YOU** !

ACKNOWLEDGMENTS

I would like to thank my **readers** for appreciating my previous publication 'Cancer to Cure'.

My heartfelt gratitude to my mother **Smt. Asha Saxena**, my husband Dr. Hari Pandey and my lovely angels Anandita and Sangeet for their constant support and love.

Thank you, dear reader for choosing this book and taking your first step towards being happy! **Welcome to your very own *Voyage to Happiness*!**

Love and Regards,
Sanchita Pandey

Chapter 1

HAPPINESS BEGINS WITH YOU!

Have you ever noticed how effortlessly an eagle glides in the sky? We too are supposed to live life the same way — light and effortlessly; in freedom and happiness.

Preparation has to start at the thought level with 'awareness' as to what kind of thoughts we entertain in our mind throughout the day. **The real test of happiness is when you smile even when nobody is around!** By thinking right thoughts, you will prevent any leakage of energy. In turn, you will be filled with positive life-giving energy.

Catering to Outside Influences

Even if you resolve to be happy encouraging right thoughts and feelings, won't outside people or circumstances influence you? For overcoming negative outside influences, one needs to be prepared in self-control, spirituality, 'no-anger' and 'let-go' traits.

Once you are connected to a higher source of power, i.e. God, you will make it a habit to pray in peace and offer all such disturbances in your life to God.

This 'outsourcing' will help you in such a way that you will become only a witness to situations, without

becoming a part of the problem yourself. You will free yourself from the bondage of anger, irritations, worry and other negative mood changes. You won't try hard to change others, but instead experience love, peace and solitude in your mind even when standing amidst a crowd.

It is also quite normal to have various moods and being sad is one of them. Some people may argue that they celebrate when something good happens in their life and are truthful enough to be sad when things go wrong in their life.

True, but then you are totally dependent on outside sources for each of your emotions! You have no control on your own self — an angry boss means your day is done today. It will be filled with sadness and not only will you crib the whole day, you will talk about the incident with your friends and repeat it in your mind the whole day...

And if this was not enough, in the evening, you will carry this burden back home. In the guise of small irritations and anger, the positive energy of your family members will be overpowered by such negative behaviour and speech. Is it worth it?

With such situations showing up nearly every day, it will become your habit to stay tense and you won't bother to smile! This in the long run will impact your health in the form of ailments like diabetes, high blood pressure, heart attacks etc.

The balm to escape all these health issues is right there *inside you*! You will not only do good to yourself but also to the world around you. **Positive vibrations and a genuine smile on your lips can heal the most distraught soul.**

"A happy person is not a person in a certain set of circumstances, but rather a person with a certain set of attitudes."
— Hugh Downs

Discover happiness for a better and cheerful life. It is very much an inherent part of you while you have been focusing outside and looking for it everywhere — in things, in situations, and in people. Let happiness be your very own nature. Be happy NOW!

I know a woman who is suffering from arthritis for some years due to which her fingers and her toes have become bent in one direction. She can hardly open her palm. But during '*teej*'— a festival in India, she wore green bangles and even put '*mehandi*' (henna tattoos) on her palms as she has always been very fond of decking up during festivals.

Her attitude is stronger than her pain and suffering of arthritis. Also, she *chose* to be happy rather than sitting and cribbing or questioning as to why she was given such a disease by God.

"If you want to lead a happy life, tie it to a goal, not to people or objects."
— Albert Einstein

So, although we may not be masters of our circumstances, we can still be masters of our happiness. Whenever you are surrounded by doubts and fear, think about all the good things life has offered you — kids, parents, eyes, brain, friends, neighbourhood etc. **Resolve to be HAPPY!**

Chapter 2

OPTIMISM VS. PESSIMISM

A man was falling down from a six-storeyed building. From one of the windows someone inquired, "How are you?" The man was an optimist to the core. He replied, "All right so far!"

In various circumstances of our life, much depends on how we perceive life-situations and how much power we give to unwelcome situations. We always wield the choice to see the glass as half empty or half full. We should make it a point not to be overawed by the unpleasant situation we are in, if any. A situation in itself is not powerful; we bestow it with power by thinking overtime about it and discussing about it. We tend to talk more about the problem than about ways to solve the problem.

When life gives you a lemon, make a lemonade! An optimist's way of thinking is to look at the silver lining in the dark black clouds. He will wait patiently for better times to come but not without trying hard all the time. When an optimist fails or falls, his belief in himself is intact and he thinks positively. His inner faith makes him get up again, try one more time and run the race of life. In the end, he wins, because he thinks he can win. He achieves success and happiness by the sheer power of his thought combined with his will power.

"What seems to us as bitter trials are often blessings in disguise."
— Oscar Wilde

You must have heard of these often-quoted lines that say, "I complained for shoes till I met a man who had no feet." You can possess all the wealth in the world and still remain unhappy.

Even in remote places where there is dearth of basic amenities of life, little children can be seen playing and merrily jumping into the village pond. Their happiness knows no bounds. They are happy in that moment and enjoying it to the fullest. They are neither in the past and nor in the future. They are living in the now and are happy with whatever life has offered them in that very moment. So, try to become a very optimistic person. It will make you radiant and you will ooze out confidence and satisfaction. The best part is that you will be a happy person. Even in times of difficulty, you will know how to adjust your sails and move on, instead of sulking and fretting. Remember, *kites fly against the wind.*

I have to convey this story again and again as it remains my favourite. It is about an old donkey which fell into a deep pit at a construction site. His master tried to save him and pull him out but unable to do so, he left him there. Soon the donkey would be buried under tons of sand that the machines were pouring into the pit. Left alone on his own, the donkey was not the one to give up so easily. Each time sand was thrown over him, he shrugged it off and stood over the heap. He kept doing this till the pit got filled up with sand and the donkey was free to go his way!

When you make it a habit to see the good in every situation, you will find a reason to always keep smiling. To be loved and be happy is the universal desire of every soul in this world. Some people may argue that optimists don't see things as they really are. They are dreamers. Mind you, if you want to make something a reality in your life, believe in it. Ask and receive it for sure. Do not ask how it will be possible. Let the Universe provide you, fulfil all your wishes and bring them forward in your life.

Being too realistic prevents you from dreaming of bigger and better things and you remain unhappy in the present moment. You see things as they are and do not visualize things as they could be.
Optimism gives hope and this hope keeps you engaged in some higher purpose in life. It gives you an elevated sense of yourself at present, till the Universe really elevates you to your desired platform in life. So, you are happy now and later, you will be happy in future too! That is what we want in life, isn't it? — happiness, lots of it.

It does not matter where you are standing right now, what matters is where you are headed to. That is to say, become a very optimistic person — actually, the most optimistic person you have ever come across should be YOU! The quality of your thoughts and the state of your mind will define how happy you are as a person.

How optimistic you are depicts how healthy, wealthy, happy and successful you will be in your life. In problems and misfortunes, get up each time and complete your racc — a race not against others but a race that makes you proud of yourself in the end — that you never gave up amidst difficulties; fell down but had the grit of getting up again and running back on track and revel in this journey called life. Happiness in your life comes from the way you think!

"The essence of optimism is that it takes no account of the present, but it is a source of inspiration, of vitality and hope where others have resigned; it enables a man to hold his head high, to claim the future for himself and not to abandon it to his enemy."
— Dietrich Bonhoeffer

You and your attitude are the source of your happiness. Beware of what inputs you give to your mind because that will decide how happy you are throughout the day today. Ignore all negative discussions and incidents. Delete them then and there. Do not repeat them again to someone else as they tend to get reaffirmed in your mind and then produce similar thoughts overtime.

One afternoon, I saw an old lady collect dry clothes. Just then a shrill voice was heard asking her not to touch the clothes as they were meant for ironing. The old woman fell down suddenly out of confusion. She raised one hand to get support from her daughter-in-law when her teenage granddaughter too arrived at the scene. None gave her any help and the poor old woman used her walking stick as a support and somehow got up silently. Both the young souls looked all around to make sure nobody saw all this.

This incident was shocking. I wanted relate it to my husband when he returned home from office in the evening but a kind of 'awareness' stopped me from reiterating the same negative incident again.

One, it would leave the atmosphere negative and that is not what a person wants to hear when he returns home tired from a full day's work. Secondly, I would be etching a negative incident in my mind not only for that day but for many days ahead. This incident would become the topic of my discussion and source of my future thoughts. I would become an envelope of negative energy posting everyone who came in contact with me this very energy. So, I deleted it then and there as if the incident never happened.

The point I want to make here is that you should think well before speaking with anyone. Speak positive things or do not speak at all. Gradually, thinking positive will become a habit and you will exude a positive aura. Keep your life simple and happiness will be yours.

"Very little is needed to make a happy life; It is all within yourself, in your way of thinking."
— Marcus Aurelius

Remember that the one person who can make you joyous and happy is YOU! You do not have to put the key to your own happiness in someone else's pocket! Yes, Happiness depends on ourselves. Mark Twain has said, "The best way to cheer yourself up is to cheer somebody else up!"

Chapter 3

BURY THE PAST

Travel light. Don't carry the additional burden of your past hurts and misses in life. **The past is dead and gone. It does not deserve the importance we give to it.** Learn from whatever mistakes you have committed.

If you feel someone else is responsible for your failure or misery, you are actually giving power to that person or incident. Forgive now and take another forward step in your life. *Don't hold on to your past. The happiest people have a very short memory indeed!*

Getting Influenced by People and Situations

We tend to get affected by people and situations and instead of burying unpleasant incidents of our past, we bury our smiles instead! A single word — *'forgiveness'* can take us to freedom, if we really practice it in our day-to-day life. *Our own bitter experiences serve as speed breakers to our happiness.*

We carry the heavy baggage of resentment in our minds against people who hurt us in some way and we drag forward in life. It may seem justified to hate someone and hold on to grudges because of what someone said or did to you; it could be a quarrel, injustice or fraud. Which road would you yourself like to travel — one full of potholes and speed breakers or a smooth-running road?

Being happy doesn't mean everything is perfect. It means that you have decided to look beyond the imperfections.

By repeating unpleasant incidents, you hurt yourself again and again. You inflict emotional pain on yourself time and again and then complain that someone else hurt you? Free yourself from this bondage of hateful and hurtful thoughts. *Be alive to the magic which the present moment can offer you.* Do your best in the work you undertake but leave the result of your efforts to the Almighty. **When we let go, we let God.**

An old lady I know swears at her daughter-in-law and son and goes to the extent of cursing them. They are staying under the same roof but they do not speak to one another. The grandma carries grudges against her daughter-in-law which date back to the time when she was married! Her complaints include petty issues like the young woman having belonged to a not-so wealthy family before her marriage and also that she was instrumental in changing the nature of her son.

Imagine the quality of vibrations that will fill the space in such a home (or is it just a house?) and the impact it will have on each individual residing in that negative space. It won't come as a surprise to you when I mention the fact that this old woman consumes not less than 8 medicines at a time.

As far as happiness in our lives is concerned, we are all human bombshells who keep attacking our own happiness by big negative balls of false egos, past hurts, jealousies, hate, feelings of revenge and impatience.

What do You Really Need to be Happy?

Nice thoughts for yourself and for others, letting go of control over others, contentment, a passion in life (which can be singing, painting, sports, swimming, writing or reading, etc.). It should be something you want to know more about, something you love to discuss with others. Such interests serve as a way of going out and mingling with other people. At least it is better than discussing office politics even when you are outside your office building.

Leave your baggage of 'what happened in office, school' etc. at the office or school gate when you leave the premises after work. **Do not carry the burden of unpleasant incidents back home. The people you were irritated about the whole day are actually present without really being present!**

So, your eyes will not be able to appreciate the good marks your child scored or the sumptuous dinner your wife has prepared. You will also miss out really looking and appreciating the lovely garden your neighbour is maintaining and the beautiful flowers that bloomed today in your little pot.

By constantly contemplating about people you detest, you give them the ticket to talk, walk and torture you by operating from the space in your mind. How will you smile if this is the case in your daily life? You will get tired carrying the burden of so many 'detestable people' (as you find them to be) with you throughout the day. I suggested this to my friend and he roared back — "You won't understand till you go through what I am going through. It is easy to preach from a distance. I speak about my office and colleagues so that I am able to vent out whatever is inside me."

Every time you relate an unpleasant incident, the obnoxious conversation robs you of gratitude, makes you a complainer, puts you in the 'victim mode' and your aura turns negative. It also reiterates the fact that yes, your office and colleagues are really bad as you are rightfully relating incidents as a proof for the same and so it is alright for you to feel miserable.

With so many issues in your day to day life, your body tissues will feel the sadness of your life and act accordingly. As a victim of your life situations, you will be proved right with the new reports on your high blood pressure, diabetes etc. Common cold will really be common for you, and the pain here and there... Well, the cycle goes on till you find yourself sitting with a bowl of medicines early in the morning every day to be consumed with breakfast. Who is to blame? Who carried the burden home? Who related one incident that happened in a span of about 15 minutes actually, 50 times after your office was over? And you were looking for happiness!

You Can Make Amends Now

It is never too late to start. Take out time for meditation, yoga, sports, brisk walking and do all your work with detachment. **You also have a personality apart from your profession. Office work is only a part of your life and you mistook it for life itself.**
Like the aforementioned grandma and friend, we too keep looking for solace, peace and good health outside of us whereas if you look closely enough, you can be the first person to gift yourself good health. Just be aware of the quality of thoughts you are entertaining.

Get rid of grudges and negativity in your thoughts by replacing them with positive thoughts. You deserve a beautiful life. Guard your happiness before you fall prey to demeaning thoughts. Don't give power to negative thoughts; instead *empower yourself.*

Happiness comes from having a 'bad memory' as far as unpleasant incidents and people are concerned. *Happiness brings good health.* When you send loving energy, the people around you will reflect the same loving positive energy towards you. You will then feel abundance of love in your life! *Remember, the change started with you!*

There is a story about a father who was busy reading the newspaper. To keep his little son engaged, he asked him to join pieces of paper which would form a globe. This was indeed difficult for the little boy but still he managed it and came back to his father rather too soon. Surprised, the father asked him how he managed to join those pieces so fast, the boy replied, "There was a photograph of a person on the reverse side of the paper. I joined the pieces to make the person properly and the image of the globe too aligned accordingly."

Write all your hurts on sand so that the winds of forgiveness can erase them with passage of time. Write all your happy moments on stone so that you can go back and read it again and again and remain in gratitude.

So true, *if we become good, the whole world will become good to us.* The vibrations of our thoughts reach a person much before we have spoken anything at all! When you remain positive, you feel nice and such positive feelings bring forward beautiful experiences in your daily life.

"Success is not the key to happiness. Happiness is the key to success. If you love what you are doing, you will be successful."
— Albert Schweitzer

Thus, be conscious of the quality of your thoughts. Don't feed your mind with negative thoughts because if you do, you will gradually start believing them!

"People are often unreasonable and self- centred.
Forgive them anyway.

If you are kind, people may accuse you of ulterior
motives.
Be kind anyway.

If you are honest, people may cheat you.
Be honest anyway.

If you find happiness, people may be jealous.
Be happy anyway.

Give the world the best you have and it may never
be enough.
Give your best anyway.

For you see, in the end, it is between you and God.
It was never between you and them anyway."

— Kent M. Keith

Chapter 4

FIRE OF ANGER

When we are angry, we are under a spell of transitory madness. Our blood pressure soars up, our voice is raised and we disobey basic courtesy. Our words are like arrows which once out of the bow, cannot be retrieved. Later, we may be surprised at what we said and how we behaved, but by then it is too late. Someone has been hurt already! By then, relationships have soured and many hearts hurt.

Anger actually causes more injury to the person who is angry than the person whom they are angry at. It causes harm to our body and mind.

"Anger is an acid that can do more harm to the vessel in which it is stored than to anything on which it is poured."

— Mark Twain

However, we can program our reactions and behaviour well in advance — before any intimidating situation crops up which can make us angry. We then derive power to *choose* our reaction. We become *aware* of our behaviour. In any situation, we learn to keep our mind stable.

Did we ever pay heed to the fact that anger does not solve any problem? It only aggravates the problem. The solution lies in keeping calm and try to find out a solution. **When**

you are angry, you give away your power. It eats away your happiness and leaves you panting, complaining and sulking. **Learn to manage difficult people and unwanted situations instead of becoming vulnerable yourself.**

"If another can easily anger you, it is because you are off balance with yourself."
— unknown

Intimidation and irritations come in our way to teach us patience. Anger is like an enemy which resides within us. To be happy, we have to uproot anger from our personality. Anger is not the only way. We can be more assertive and loving and get our work done. But anger, in most circumstances, cannot be justified.

You can be as cool as a cucumber or burn as coal. The latter will leave you devastated and tired. It will sour your relationships and you will be an easy target of intimidation. You will be prone to irritations and intimidations throughout the day.

Getting angry more often will become a habit and then even without giving another thought, you will become a person who is seen shouting at others and later sorry for your wrong behaviour and offensive words!

"You will not be punished for your anger, you will be punished by your anger."
— Buddha

It is possible that the other person is so spiritually elevated that he did not 'receive' your angry words and forgave you then and there. In such a case, imagine the damage you did to your mind and body which bore 100% of the brunt of your anger. **Your anger is self-damaging.** We complain and criticize the whole world while **we ourselves are our own worst enemy when we are angry.**

Program your mind in advance as to how you will react in a certain situation — that you will *not get angry or irritated*. Even if you are not successful in controlling anger a few times in the beginning, do not lose heart. Program your mind again for such incidents and visualize how you will react in future. When such a situation arises, you will automatically become *aware* of your emotional changes in the unpleasant situation. Also, you will be able to practice restraint and self-control so that the situation will be taken care of peacefully. You will now enjoy a new and better version of yourself, feel like a winner and be in peace.

"Holding on to anger is like drinking poison and expecting the other person to die."
— Buddha

Anger is definitely a blocking stone towards a happy life. When will you live your precious happy moments? We keep planning everything for the future: when my baby grows up, when I lose this extra flab, when I shift to a new place.... STOP! The right time is now. **NOW**.

Learn to Enjoy the Dualities of Life

All your trials and tribulations are your life itself. Then, what are you waiting for? Life will come to meet you each moment as a pair. That means, just like there is night after day, there is winter to summer and there is light to darkness, your life too will have duality throughout. That explains why we have a combo deal for joy and sorrow. Never cling to one.

Practice equanimity in cheer and despair. They are two sides of the same coin called life. One follows the other and none is permanent. Laugh heartily when you are happy and cry when you are sad. But always remember that your good times are just round the corner. A truly happy person knows this fact and even in sadness, keeps a happy countenance because he can visualize the presence of happiness in the nearest corner of this journey of life. Such a person knows no stress, anger, depression and lethargy. He will be full of love and that is all he has to give others.

Someone asked me —

How can a person suffering from any disease remain happy?
Yes, it is possible for him by believing that he is fine and cured already. Belief in the power of your own subconscious mind can work wonders. *Choose* to think that you are recovered and visualize your own picture about how you are giving this happy news to your friends and relatives. *Pray and meditate instead of worrying and sulking.* There are many patients who have cured themselves by adopting a more disciplined lifestyle, exercising and consuming a healthy diet.

How can a person confined in jail be happy?
Remember that in-between the external stimulus and you, there is a thin gap where you can choose your reaction to any particular situation. You can choose to be in peace,

forgive others who hurt you, engage yourself in fruitful skills and pray a lot. Let go off the past hurts and look forward towards making your life more peaceful and purposeful.

There are so many people out there walking in freedom but actually are 'prisoners' of their previous hurts, sorrows and even future ambitions. They fail to enjoy their 'present' and either crib about their past or burn with the desire to succeed in future. **The way to be happy is to live in the moment and cherish whatever you have while striving to work hard for future success.**

Be happy first and then work to succeed.

Resolve to be happy today, no matter what life brings for you. **There is an opportunity in every adversity.** Look for the brighter side. *Ignore people who bring in negativity in your life.* Give time to those who fill your life with enthusiasm and happiness. Appreciate what you like today, be with nature. Try to learn something new each day as this will keep you cheerful and yes, do follow your heart — keep a few moments every day for hobbies you love. It can be music, painting, sports or just hitting the gym. Happiness will remain your perpetual friend only if you give her a nice dwelling place in your heart. Keep the road to your heart clean — devoid of speed-breakers of anger, lust, revenge, complaining attitude etc. The accessibility should be such that everyone reaches straight to the core of your heart and bathes in the nectar of your love.

You can bring love and cheer in another person's life only if you are yourself cheerful. Remove any anger from your heart because you actually hurt yourself with your anger. A wise person is never angry and yes, his anger is too expensive to get! A quick temper will sooner or later be detrimental to your success. Manage your irritations and anger well in advance by programming your mind not to suddenly react to situations. The best person to start working for and working with is actually YOU!

Chapter 5

FREEDOM FROM FEAR

If we analyze carefully, most of our enemies are not anywhere beyond our own selves! Fear, anger, guilt, jealousy etc. are some of them. Fear is at the top of the list because **we not only fear the real things in life but also fictitious things.** Certain fears never show up in our life but we fear them throughout our lives — fictitious fears. There is no enemy stopping us. We become our own worst enemy by being engulfed in *"What if..."*

Initially, when I enrolled in a computer course, we were being taught computer programming. The whole thing seemed like some foreign language, difficult to understand. I felt like quitting but my husband encouraged me and prompted me not to lose hope. "Man has invented computer and today you yourself are afraid of it?" This made me understand my folly. It was only fear that was conditioning me to follow the already tread path and not venture into something new. I went back to my classes with renewed vigor, thinking of this man-made machine as my slave which would follow my instructions. My fear was gone and I started looking forward to attend my classes every day. I completed the post graduate course with a good 70% marks and 'excellent' remark for my computer project.

Life is like a big classroom. We should learn our lessons, make amends and then move on. Real failure is to stop midway, to accept defeat for fear of failure. Every seed that you plant in life does not grow into a tree. But, keep on planting seeds. Don't stop. Do it even if you fear it. **Let not fear set limits for you.** Later in life, *you will be proud of all the things you ventured for rather than did not try at all.*

There is also fear of disease and death. Even if you are not well today, do not fear hospitalization or death. Instead, think positive about yourself and visualize yourself as improving and being healthy and do all the things you love to do. Each thought reaches the Universe and is granted just like prayers.

Keep the candle of hope burning and curb your fear. Be confident that only the best will be given to you; only the very best will happen to you. Difficult situations in life are only hurdles which should make you leap to further greatness and success in life. **Run your own race. Fear also creeps in when we compare ourselves too much with others.**

I know an old man 89 years of age who boards a bus, gets off at the bus stand and further walks a couple of kilometers to reach our house, just to greet us!

Another old woman I know goes to the hospital all alone, gets her medicines and walks back home using her walker. If she is lucky someday, an auto gives her a lift half distance till the main road and she walks back home not less than a kilometer. I have always admired her grit.

Yet another person I appreciate is about 85 years old but still drives his car, plays table tennis and even runs to pick the ball and is involved with social service for the needy. These individuals are confident and do not think of old age as a limitation for anything they want to do. *They have acquired victory over their fears. You too can, starting from NOW.*

There is fear of what people will think, of being judged. Take life in your stride. Take life as it comes. Keep in mind that there is always another way. Work on your fear and it will automatically disappear. Only then will you reach your true potential in life. Banish this Satan of fear from your mind. Live in the present moment. That is all you have now. Why let the fear of tomorrow ruin your today? **Live each precious moment NOW.**

No Fear
No Limits
No Excuses

When my daughter started learning swimming, she was very scared. Seeing the coach approaching, she used to dip her head under water so that he would not notice her. But one day, the coach caught hold of her and in no time, she started yelling out of fear!

Everyone present there stared at her in surprise. My daughter was so afraid she was trembling. She thought that she would drown and so started crying loudly. The coach remained unperturbed, held her hands gently and gave instructions. After a while my daughter was seen swimming on her own, albeit for a short distance, but those fearful looks on her face had vanished.

Now there was thrill and a sense of achievement in her eyes! She was the same person with a different attitude. Really, *'Darr ke aage jeet hai'* (Get rid of your fears and victory is yours). How true!

Chapter 6

EACH DAY IS A FESTIVAL

We get what we focus on. If we focus on negative incidents of our life, that is what we will receive more in life. If we learn and practice to forgive and forget the unpleasant incidents, we will not experience emotions of hatred, anger, revenge and jealousy and will move much, much ahead in life — towards happiness.

Life can either be a festival or just a drudgery. It depends on the world we create within ourselves. Hell and heaven are not any outside places. They are present inside us and accordingly, we come across outside situations in life.

If, for instance, I think about negative experiences, my behaviour will be one of fear, suspicion and hate. I will attract similar people and situations all around me. If, on the other hand, I carry loving and peaceful thoughts, that's where I will be placed.

One must learn from various experiences and move on in life. To go along with the flow of life, we should not even go into the good and bad of incidents and accept life situations as they show up. Instead of weaving stories around situations, we should learn to *just be*.

Each day is a little lifetime.
Enjoy every moment.

Once we align ourselves with the flow of life, we will start living and working from a deeper space within ourselves and be peaceful and happy too. To lead a beautiful life of abundance and happiness, try to encourage only beautiful experiences in your mind; replace judgmental and negative thoughts with nice and loving thoughts, say, when you won a prize, when you received the trophy for sports, when you got your much coveted promotion, the day you were married or just think of your lovely kids. You will be surprised to find yourself experiencing such beautiful moments everyday with some interesting people all around you. Your life has become heaven! It is so simple.

When happy people are confronted with sorrow or disease in their life, their inner light shines through, their faith in the Almighty takes over and they steer across difficult times with ease. We should make it a point to see the 'good' in any situation. If you are ill, be happy that at least you are able to attend office. If you are bedridden, be happy that you are alive and near your family members and kids. Let not any sort of failure stop you; get up one more time and take one step ahead with confidence.

To be happy, take some time to think about others. Learn to appreciate.
A few loving words can make someone's day. Give a gift of kind words showing your gratitude for someone you love. Can you imagine that the person will go back home and repeat to his family about what you said so lovingly!

Speak well of others, steer away from negative speech and arguments and try to be non-judgmental in your approach. People will be different and they may not necessarily conform to the image you have made up in your mind about them. So what? Enjoy their imperfections, love the fact that they are different from you!

Just love others for what they are and not what you want them to be. You will be more at peace with yourself and with others. Peace and joy will bring happiness in your life. Give yourself a gift — play, dance, go out shopping, walking or cycling, play with your pet, just surf the net, read your favourite book, sing and just be with yourself. Enjoy doing what you love doing the most.

Celebrate life and live your life to the fullest potential. Every day will become a festival of joy for you! The idea is to give yourself some time so that you are able to connect with yourself first! If you are happy, only then you can spread happiness. How can you give others what you yourself do not possess?

Take care of yourself. Get the latest haircut, buy a pair of nice shoes, a colourful and trendy dress/shirt, bag and look well groomed. A thing of beauty is a joy forever. *Little things can bring happiness into our lives when we just keep chasing bigger, distant dreams and goals!*

When you smile at others, you make the other person happy. This emotion percolates to your own being reiterating the fact that you too are a happy person in this moment — in the NOW. So, a little smile is not only a great service to mankind but an equally great service done for your own self! **Let happiness start from you.** A smile is free, requires only a few muscles but is still so rare. It not only glows your own world but lightens up the lives of others too. So, genuinely smile, appreciate, compliment, hug and pat others more often. Make them feel good and in turn enjoy moments of happiness yourself!

Chapter 7

POSITIVE SELF-AFFIRMATION

The greatest source of energy in our everyday life is when we keep connected to the Almighty and offer our work to Him. A large part of positive energy is also derived from the conversation we have with ourselves (in our mind) throughout the day.

We should build a positive picture of ourselves in our own minds. No failure is final. Even if we fall down, we still have an option to stand up and continue the race. **We are not defeated till we have hope.** Positive self-affirmation builds up our energy and we feel encouraged to keep up our efforts.

Even when you are unwell, say to yourself that you are fine, you are healthy and take care of yourself. That is the message your subconscious mind will send to your body and you will be healed faster.

One fine day, I just decided to 'observe' everyone I met and the way they responded when I greeted them. Early in the morning, I met an old lady sitting silently and basking in the morning sun.

"How are you?" I enquired.

It was as if I had dug up deep hurts within her! So, off she started on how her grandchildren were nasty and misbehaved with her all the time and broke her cupboard handle, how she was contemplating a change of place to dwell anywhere other than where she was putting up presently...

When I reached home, my phone was already ringing. "Hi, nice to hear your voice after such a long time," I exclaimed recognizing my friend's voice. Yes, of course, said she and with this started a list of complaints!

These experiences really made me wonder as to what happiness really was all about. Is it absence of problems in life, or how we perceive the various situations we are in?

Is Happiness an Attitude Only?

It is a pleasure to receive the young woman who comes everyday to clean my house. She is a working woman too with three children to take care of, all studying in various grades. She enters like a wave of fresh air and has a warm smile. She is not rich but hardworking and contented. True, **there is enough in everyone's life at least to smile once in a day.** Reiterate in your mind even in the worst of situations, "Yes, I can do it." God is with me and He is the greatest power. So, I have no fear.

"Be careful how you are talking to yourself because you are listening."
— Lisa M. Hayes

When I was in college, sitting for an audition in an auditorium, I was rather repenting why I did not learn classical music while I was young. Each time a younger participant turned up on stage and sang a difficult song well, my heart sank deeper and deeper in sorrow.

Then suddenly I felt a ray of hope. "Hey," I said to myself, "why can't I learn now? Why not when I am in college? Why can't I begin now?" It was just the conditioning of my mind that I had to change. And lo! I was elated and full of cheer suddenly… I was *happy*!

I enrolled for a degree course in music, practiced and learnt well and even won a number of music competitions. *More than anything, I was a winner in my own eyes. My soul felt satisfied.* I feel so happy, even today, that I followed the passion of my soul. This is to say, **in life, we build our own barriers most of the time.**

Positive self-affirmation works wonders for our health too. It is like life-giving energy, making you radiant and giving you a 'purpose' in life to do everything well — whatever you undertake to do.

Practice non-judgment in your interaction with others. Try to accept others *as they are* and not *as we want them to be.* However, it is fine to steer away from pessimistic people or those who tend to put all their problems on your shoulders as that can drain your own energy.

It is essential that you take care of what inputs you are giving to your mind because the output of thoughts in your mind will be directly proportional to such inputs. That is why it is a good idea not to read newspapers early in the morning. Morning time should be reserved for yoga, meditation, spiritual or motivational books and prayer so that you 'charge your battery' for the whole day.

Newspapers are filled more with negative news than positive, which tend to play in our minds throughout the day. This way, we will start our day with a negative approach towards life, which is not right.

Positive self-affirmation means positive self-talk with yourself. Don't start blaming yourself when you fall sick or fail. Detach from the disease or incident and see it as separate from yourself. Then only will you be able to manage the situation and find a feasible solution.

We believe what we tell ourselves.

Do not say things like 'it always happens with me', 'I am not worth anything', 'I am such a burden', 'my family has to suffer because of me', etc. You are on the *wrong* path if you practice self-pity.

Remember, you are God's own child and he loves you even more when He finds you stranded in a problem. He will give you the best in life. Only, we are unable to comprehend this during trying times. Have patience and the wheel will turn in your favour— be it financial problems, health issues or any other thing.

Be confident in the thick and thin of life. Remember, this is life! Difficulties make you strong and you will be surprised at your own grit and resilience during such times. **Difficult times are ways to know and understand yourself and others in a better way.**

Positive self-affirmation has cured ailments like cancer, diabetes, etc. and has turned average students into toppers! **Draw your own beautiful picture of life. There will be shades of grey but there will also be the long and colourful rainbow.** Don't give in to thoughts that pull your spirits down. Live life. Live in this moment. Don't just survive. Each moment is a precious gift to us. *Positive self-affirmation is the key to success and happiness in life.*

It is considered very normal to be busy, not smiling and hurrying away for school or to work. So, it is natural to see such beings everywhere. Now, all of a sudden, if in this majority, they find you jovial and happy, with a twinkle in your eyes, vivacious and energetic, eyebrows will be raised automatically. When you appear cool and happy, people think either something is wrong with you or you are in love! You can even observe the surprise on their faces. Try it out if you doubt my statement.

People find it difficult to believe that in today's times, someone can be really happy. For them, being happy is more of a joke than a reality. The general belief is that when you have a problem, you ought to look depressed and walk slowly and sadly. And everyone has some problem or the other. Hence, you can rarely find happy people around you. Why not become one yourself and spread happiness everywhere you go?

Happiness is a myth today. But then, this our own conditioning. Nobody told us not to be happy. Today, we are just 'not happy' and we do not know why. And to think that we are all working hard to be actually comfortable, financially independent, save for our future needs and family and *be happy*, not hopeless.

"A strong, positive self-image is the best possible preparation for success."
— Joyce Brothers

Initially, we don't have neither the inclination nor the time to gauge if our work, relationships or friends are giving us happiness. Later in life, we fail to be happy because we have lifelong companions in the guise of diseases and stress. Learn to love yourself unconditionally...

Love yourself first and everything else falls into place.

Today I encountered a few questions. They came like a test for me and I had to find proper solutions for each of these enquiries. **These are real problems faced by some of our own friends:**

- How will I ask a person who is suddenly unable to walk and confined strictly to bed, to be happy?

- How will I ask a friend who lost one eye due to infection after a cataract operation, to be happy?

- How will I ask a person suffering from any disease to lead a joyful life?

Let me answer these one at a time. In the first case, the friend in question is not able to get up at all and can't go to work. He is a contractor by profession and has many people working under him, has to take care of safety standards for his workers etc. when they are working on a high-rise building or in the factory. He has to claim payments from various offices for his work and also pay his workers in time, and he has his family to take care of.

Our friend has two options. One is to think that his is a hopeless case and a slap from God. He can blame the stress for his problem and can go into depression seeing that he is lying on bed with nowhere to go. He can vent his anger on others and stop meeting and greeting people. But there is another way which needs will-power and discipline. This path can keep him hopeful and happy now and later in life and will assist him in recuperation too.

Our dear friend should become prayerful to keep his mind in peace. Prayers bring blessings to you. **Prayers give you hope to cope**. The very thought that this is only a passing phase will keep him hopeful now and such positive feelings will really cure him. So, it will be happiness for now and also happiness in the future!

The second case is indeed a very sorry one. But our friend has to be bold and *'accept the isness of what is'*. The truth is that his one eye has been removed and he has to live the rest of his life with this feeling. Such a feeling can break the morale of any individual quite easily and lead him into emotions of anger for the hospital or hatred for the doctor.

He may blame the whole medical system and even not spare himself by blaming his destiny. But is it a solution? The truth is that his eye is lost and he should focus on how he will live the rest of his life — in anguish and repentance as to why he went for this operation at all? Any change in lifestyle and way of thinking needs lot of will power.

Our friend should now do the reverse! He should start rejoicing now! He has nothing to lose. He should go all out and enjoy his life. He can at least walk! He should focus on what all he has at present and still be in gratitude. This will require tremendous will power.

We are so conditioned to focus only on things which we don't have or want to achieve in the future. My advice to him would be — satisfy your soul. Dance, paint, go for excursions, sing — all without inhibitions. *Turn the tables in your favour. Dine but don't whine.*

Anyway, cribbing won't give back your eye and won't make you look any better. But a radiant smile will!

People are attracted towards happy people and they will be inspired by them to live life joyfully. Your family will be happy because you are happy. The past will not ruin your future and instead make you a better and jovial person.

Easier said than done? Not at all. Last year, I cried like a child when my husband returned from the office with hospital papers in which he had been diagnosed with cancer. I felt that all of a sudden, we had fallen from the top of a mountain and hit its bottom. I cried the whole night like a child punished by God: this is how I perceived my situation. But a total about-turn of attitude happened when I read about *'Quantum mind'*. This is something I wrote about in my previous book. It was like a magic formula given to me!

What Is Meant By 'Quantum Mind'?

According to 'Quantum mind', you have to engage with only positive thoughts in your mind. As soon as any negative thought passes your mind, discourage it by meditating on any other positive and happy topic. Reaffirm in your mind that you are fine and with time, everything will be alright. Do not think about past or future, remove all fears and practice being happy in that particular moment. It is just a matter of making a good choice. Choose to be HAPPY!

Trying times reflect (to you and to others) the tough person that you actually are. Take everything in your stride. Never be bogged down by difficulties. Also, don't wait to live your life in the future. Enjoy NOW amidst all your difficulties because life comes in shades of all colours.

And to tell you how happiness works miracles, my husband and I are absolutely doing fine because we chose to smile, sing, play, learn and work hard in our profession. The universe rewarded us with more happiness and abundance we could think of! We must try to spread happiness all around because being happy makes you feel so light in this journey called life.

Can you pour from an empty cup? No! This is why take care of yourself, love yourself, say positive things about yourself in your mind, be happy all day long to give happiness and appreciation to others.

Accept Yourself
Value Yourself
Forgive Yourself
Bless Yourself
Express Yourself
Trust Yourself
Bless Yourself
Love Yourself
Empower Yourself
Be Yourself !

Chapter 8

POWER OF GRATITUDE IN LIFE

Gratitude is something we all should have the most in our lives but is actually seen the least! How many times do we remember a person for his good qualities? We are adept at focusing at the negatives in our lives. We judge people and places on the basis of all the 'minus points' we can see and imagine. Such a picture gets saved in our memory and then all our future interactions with those persons or places depend on this conditioned notion which is negative!

Office gossip is also about people and is seldom positive. We make our own life and that of others always open to judgment, thereby causing stress for ourselves and also for others.

It is not happy people who are thankful. It is the thankful people who are happy.

We become so used to all that we already have that we take these things for granted instead of being thankful for them. True, *"God gives and forgives, man gets and forgets"*. How do we start feeling and showing gratitude in our lives?

Cultivate the Attitude of Gratitude

Start your day with prayer and thank the morning Sun for giving light and heat to the world. Life thrives on this

Earth because of the Sun. We should be grateful for having a loving family. We should be grateful for the gifts of good health, work, loving friends and for all worthy things in our life. We should thank the Creator for the miracles of nature in the form of beautiful plants, trees and fruits, butterflies and flowers.

Even nature has hidden lessons for mankind underneath its silent saga. The trees teach us to give without discrimination, the seasons proclaim that time keeps changing for the better and the vastness of the sky bears the amount of love we should hold in our hearts for everyone we come across throughout the day.

We keep focus on the future and so don't enjoy the NOW of our life. Every happiness, togetherness and playfulness that our life brings forward is postponed for the future. The present moment is reserved to be focused on judgment, gossip, problems, finding deficiencies and cribbing.

"Enjoy the little things, for one day you may look back and realize they were the big things."
— Robert Brault

A few days back, I bought a beautiful maroon and golden *churidaar kurta* (Indian dress) and resolved to wear it whenever we were invited to a party or any function. My daughters told me about their PTA meeting (when parents and teachers meet) in school and I was more than delighted as I would now get a chance to wear my new dress with matching new sandals and necklace! Before I went off to sleep, I joked that I was actually more interested about wearing my new dress to school than to know about what their teachers had to say about them or their rank in the class!

In the middle of the night, from nowhere, an insect with a hard body crust got into my ear. I pressed my ear to stop it from entering further inside, but could feel it struggling inside. It was going further inside my ear and now it hurt, too.

I jammed the inner portion of my ear by pressing it from the outside and pulled my ear to one side to broaden the passage, thinking that the insect could come out somehow. The pain was excruciating and fearful for me. I called out to God with my whole heart and prayed to Him to help me. All this while my daughters asked me if I was alright and my husband rushed for the ear drops.

Within five seconds of my prayer, the insect moved out of my ear and fell on the floor. I thanked God for helping me and relieving me from pain. I put antibiotic ear drops for relief from some mild pain later.

Early in the morning, on cleaning my ear I saw blood on the ear buds. I folded my hands in gratitude and prayed to God. I was so thankful for the fact that the insect did not enter my daughters' ears. I wore my new dress to school, but throughout, I had this awareness that I was walking across the school corridor and talking to teachers and my friends there, because of timely help from God. I thanked Him again and again silently when my girls complemented me for my new dress. It was by the will of the Lord that I was a part of the school meeting.

My little angels had fared well in exams. We were happy as they had filled the cup of our life with love and were so talented in drawing, sketching, singing, reciting poems, composing poems and making us laugh by narrating to us anecdotes about their friends and teachers. Need we ask more?

"Trade your expectations for appreciation and your whole world changes in an instant."
— Tony Robbins

Each moment we are together with our family, friends, enjoying dinner or going out on a picnic, we should comprehend them as gifts of God to us. We must cherish these moments and thank God that we are all fine. We can only be happy when everyone around us is joyful and fine.

We should make it our habit to remain in gratitude and avoid taking the good things of life for granted. **We should be in gratitude for all the happy moments of our life.** It is the Almighty who brings opportunities in our lives and gives us good health and good sense to work for them. Remaining in gratitude should be the *mantra* of our life.

I remember the evening when I was strolling with tears in my eyes asking God why even after one and a half years of our marriage, we did not have a child. God listened to our prayers and we are parents of two little angels who are powerhouses of talent and intelligence.

"If the only prayer you said in your whole life was 'thank you', that would suffice."
— Melster Echart

My eldest daughter had chord around her neck during birth. A watchful lady doctor ordered for Cesarean Section at the right time and my daughter was born a healthy child. I remember how I had kept my hand on my big round stomach and patted lightly whispering to the baby to come out alright. I had also promised myself that I would never scold her, no matter how naughty she acted!

I am fully in gratitude for *what is* in my life. My prayers have always been answered by the Almighty and I am grateful for this. I owe each smile and laughter to Him. I owe my achievements and talents I can be proud of, to Him. I offer all my successes, trials and errors to Him for He knows what is best for me at any given time. Thank You, O Lord, for everything!

With so many nursing homes and hospitals in every town, if you are not admitted in one of these 'body garages', you are fortunate. Be merry and dance with joy that you are breathing the air flowing outside the hospital premises.

Like a robot, keep connection with God and remain fully charged. Be in total control of your own emotions but give others the freedom to choose and be themselves.

Whether you are thinking about your friends, or your office or relatives, make it a habit to always be in gratitude. People will be attracted to you for your positive attitude. They will love you for always smiling and never harbouring ill-will against anyone.

"Perfection is a disease of a nation. We overlay our faces with tons of make-up. We get Botox and even starve ourselves to become that perfect size. We try to fix something.... but you can't fix what you can't see. It's the soul that needs the surgery. It's time that we

take a stand. How can you expect someone else to love you if you don't love yourself? You have to be happy with yourself. It doesn't matter what you look like on the outside, it's what is on the inside that counts. Today, I want to put up a makeup-free photo. I know I have wrinkles on my skin but today I want you to see beyond that. I want to embrace the real me and I want you to embrace who you are, the way you are, and love yourself just the way you are."

— Julia Roberts

I had begun to crib about why I had a sore throat the other day just when I saw a man using gestures to convey his message at the club. I learnt my lesson to be in gratitude.

Gratitude brings more good things into your life. Actually, happiness in itself is a kind of gratitude. Be thankful for everything you have because the vibration of gratitude has the power to attract more and more positive things and people into your life.

Start each day with a grateful heart!

Yes, when you are in gratitude, your whole attitude towards people and life changes. **With gratitude, you change a simple meal into a feast, your house into a lovely home and friends into a family!** Say thank you for a beautiful life and **be grateful for the small things of life which are miracles we have actually got used to.** Gratitude banishes negativity from your life, brings happiness and you start living in abundance and attract more love and prosperity because of the way you think about your life.

So, fill the cup of your life with kindness, love, understanding, hope, peace and yes, gratitude! Say "Thank you, thank you, thank you" every night before going off to sleep and see the difference it will bring to your life — abundance, happiness and prosperity.

Chapter 9

SUBSTITUTE WORRY WITH PRAYER

The amount of time we give for worrying in our life should actually be given to prayer. By praying, we will tackle our own emotions as well as the problem at hand with ease. **Prayers go up and bring blessings for us.** God is always looking at us. However, we get entangled in day-to-day activities and forget Him. We just have to tune to Him and we will feel His presence. What will worry give you anyway? How can worry help us during difficult times? **Prayer comes as a balm and hope during tough times.**

My sister relished coconut water and also got some packed for home from a street vendor. Before driving off, suddenly she realized that she had not made the payment. She got off from her car and paying the requisite sum, asked the old vendor, "Had I not paid you and driven off, would you run after me?"
"Why should I?" replied the vendor and continued, "Can anyone take away my destiny from me? I will get what is meant for me. It is He who gives, not you or me." My sister was actually quenched with this flow of enlightenment coming from a humble vendor.

While doing our work, we should remain prayerful and offer our work to the Almighty. If the 'doer' ship is His, He will also take care of the outcome. Worry will only make us sick and morose. It pulls away the smile from our faces and also affects those around us in a negative way.

There are hundred reasons to worry but the only way to keep out of this 'net' of worry is to pray. If we lose ourselves in helping others, encouraging others and doing little things of kindness which bring a smile on the faces of those who come in contact with us, where will be the time to worry? Doing good for others will also make us feel good about ourselves.

My daughters look so happy when I sit with them and help them with their homework, help them to write essays, assist them in packing their bags (finding their books, precisely!) or compliment them for studying well. One can notice the sense of achievement in their innocent eyes and their happiness makes me feel good. Worry also means that somewhere you are lacking in faith. **Where there is faith, worry cannot reside** — faith in yourself and faith in God. Even the birds start singing much before dawn. *Use obstacles to move forward, get experience and become a stronger person.*

"Times of great calamity and confusion have ever been productive of the greatest minds. The purest ore is produced from the hottest furnace, and the brightest thunderbolt is elicited from the darkest storm."
— Charles Caleb Colton

Worry doesn't let us enjoy our precious moments of life today. **When we worry, any acknowledgement of beauty and happiness is postponed for later times** and we burn in anguish. We always have a choice — either we can sit and worry, sapping not only our own energy but also that of others— or we can have faith and patiently wait while at the same time doing our bit in the given situation.

A single shift in our thought can change the way we are living our life and also our perception of the problem at hand. Either rise above the difficulty or be bogged down by it. But a little positive effort on your part can open new doors of hope, support, opportunities and love from your near and dear ones.

We design our own happiness by the way we think. So, make it your habit to think only positive thoughts, ignore the negative inputs from people and situations and avoid repeating them to others or to yourself.

All nice and beautiful things happen in your life when you get rid of negative thoughts. The quality of your life depends upon the quality of thoughts you entertain in your mind. Fill your mind with good and beautiful thoughts, love for yourself and others. Pray to God and remain ever happy. Keep your mind stable and cool in all circumstances. Start NOW. **Smile at your mistakes, learn from them and move on in life.** Turn over a new leaf in your life and start living anew.

Look for new and better ways of solving your problem and have confidence in yourself. **Worry will not take away your sorrows, it will empty today of its strengths!**

Chapter 10

SURRENDER: THIS TOO SHALL PASS!

During tough times, when we experience feelings of loneliness or sorrow, the way to energize ourselves is — acceptance. Failure, death or disease tear us apart. Acceptance makes you come to terms with any kind of loss and leads you into thinking what needs to be done in future; it leads you towards a solution rather than contemplation on 'Why this? *Why me?*' thinking pattern. You slow down and your meditative mind takes you to your own self— the self which you never connected with earlier. That is why they say that wounds are windows that lead you to yourself.

When you are at peace with yourself, you find and connect with your true Father and creator— GOD. Henceforth, you are never alone. You have now tuned in towards the reservoir of power and positive energy which will keep you rejuvenated and happy.

Now, all your trials and tribulations become HIS. **He will show you the path, make one if need be, and deliver all that you need just in time.** He is the Divine energy that controls the universe. Ask and receive. Believe in Him. Surrender to Him.

"I surrender... I will trust your plan for my life."

— MATTHEW 6:31-34

Our tensions on what will happen in the future do not let us live in this precious present moment. **Each moment passes by and we do not even realize this. What we ought to cherish, we actually perish!** Every moment is like a gem bestowed to us by our Father in heaven to smile and be joyful. Be in the present moment and surrender to God. Keep your faith unto Him that only the very best will happen to you. **When you surrender, God steps in for you and takes charge.** Go with the natural flow of life. If you perceive carefully, all the work is done in nature silently and orderly — the unfolding of a flower, the falling of teeth when children are young, the transformation of a caterpillar into a beautiful butterfly... Each bird gets its food every day, by the grace of God. So, the next step involves — **letting go**.

Think only positive thoughts and go with the natural flow of life. *Surrender your questions, anxieties, sorrow, inhibitions, anger, repentance — everything to God.* Now, instead of messing up and creating more agony for yourself, you walk towards solution and peace.

God's grace is seldom early, but *never* late.

Here is a story for you. A devotee of Lord Shiva suddenly had a fight with a friend. Lord Shiva saw this from heaven. To protect his devotee, he got up to go and rescue him. Then, suddenly he sat down and started meditating again. His wife, Parvati, asked him, "Are you not going to rescue your ardent devotee?" Shiva replied, "Yes, I was going for this reason only. But now he himself has picked up a stone to defend himself. He doesn't need me."

Sometimes, *just be*. Do not think or worry, do not get angry under stress. Just pray and keep your faith in the Lord. **Have patience and see how well things will work out for you!**

The act of surrendering gives you hope and confidence that there is superior power up there who is taking care of you. You become sure that individual care is being given to you and God is working on your case. So, only the best will happen to you, your prayers will be answered; this is but a passing phase. Just see it pass. **Above the clouds, the sun is still shining brightly. Wait for your happy days and they will be given back to you.**

Setbacks and sorrow connect us with ourselves and with God. They realign us on the spiritual path of inner joy, peace and enlightenment. You discover your true self and slow down. You become compassionate and understanding towards others. You become a better human being. You have a greater connection with God.

I used to pray earlier too. But now when I pray, I am filled with gratitude towards God for coming to our rescue in difficult times. So, my prayer is such that I am totally into it, with more concentration and more love towards Him. **While praying, this universe is reduced to having only Him and me, praying ardently to my Father in heaven.**

"When trouble comes, focus on God's ability to care for you."
— Charles Stanley

Hold on to the one and *only power* in the universe— God. ***Surrender to God.* By surrendering, automatically, the**

onus of your happiness and well-being shifts on God. He is the supreme power and will hold you in His palms and protect you. What's more, you can now enjoy a nice, peaceful sleep! Your Father in heaven is working for you. Have faith and surrender, surrender, surrender to God.

*"What is the difference
Between your experience of Existence
And that of a Saint?
The saint knows
That the spiritual path
Is a sublime chess game with God
And that the Beloved
Has just made such a Fantastic Move.
That the saint is now continually
Tripping over Joy
And bursting out in Laughter
And saying, 'I Surrender!'
Whereas, my dear,
I am afraid you still think
You have a thousand serious moves."*

— Hafiz,
*I Heard God Laughing;
Poems of Hope and Joy*

Chapter 11

TAKE TO SPORTS

Sports is a minimized version of life itself. One should take to sports early in life. We are taught to be competitive. We learn various ways to win in life but no one teaches how to take defeat in your own stride or how to lose gracefully. When you play any sport you learn discipline, you learn to understand and plan your moves beforehand and focus on your positive aspects in the game.

Sports Teaches You Equanimity

Any sport is about attitude, practice and positive reaffirmation. So is life. Life is a continuous game. Getting a degree from the best college, getting married to the most accomplished person, laying your hands on the biggest bungalow in town or becoming a CEO at a young age doesn't end the race.

You have to go beyond the red ribbon to define success. It's about how well you know yourself, how loving, giving and forgiving have you been to others and how happy you are as an individual.

Have you been a friend to yourself? Or have you just run the race mechanically following instructions and dying to reach the end without knowing that the pleasure lay in enjoying the journey itself!

I know of a woman who participated in a Table Tennis (T.T.) tournament and never ever returned to the T.T. room after she was defeated in the annual tournament, which she had never lost before. **Fight if you must, work hard, give your best but never quit in the face of difficulty.** If you face defeat, practice, learn and come back again to play your best game. Only then you are a real champion. This is something we learn by playing any sport.

How A Winner Gets Defeated...

Shyamli was an intelligent girl who always stood first in her class. Gradually, it dawned to her that the first position was her right and so, without even realizing, got attached to the result.

True, she worked hard, impressed her teachers and made sure she knew everything about what her competitors were doing before and during the examination. If they went for extra classes or better teachers for tuition, she worked harder. The end was important: she *had* to stand first in her class. Each time she made it to the first position, it reaffirmed the belief that second position was not good; the second position meant that you have been defeated. While everyone appreciated her for winning, no one taught her how to lose... and try again... one more time... another time. In the Board exams in class X, the answer sheets were checked by external teachers and Shyamli did come second in her class.

Shyamli could have taken solace from the fact that around four students had failed in her class who would have to repeat in the same class. Few of her classmates had to repeat a couple of papers. They had to redefine their strategy and go back to the track to continue the race. It was after all a passing phase, an unwelcome failure, a learning experience to study harder and try one more time. But Shyamli took it to her heart. Her life and first position had become synonymous. Her happiness lay in coming first only and this is where she got entangled in life's net. We were taken aback by the news of her suicide a few days later.

Stumbling in Life Only to Rise Again

Pratibha always participated in 400- and 800-meter races on Sports Day. For two consecutive years, she did not win but kept participating just to make sure that she completed the race and did not leave halfway. As a married woman, when her husband was detected with cancer, the grit that lay dormant in her resurfaced and she worked hard, accompanied her husband everyday to the hospital, loved him more, prayed more with the unflinching belief that he would be totally cured one day. And true, her husband did become absolutely alright!

He actually enjoyed better health than he ever did as he became disciplined. He started taking care of himself by avoiding any beverages, artificial drinks, fast food, going for regular walks and maintaining a perfect body weight. **A stumble in life did not topple them down but instead brought their best forward.**

What is the difference between these two stories?

Remember, no player can be greater than the game! Accept defeat and move forward. Be happy and **believe that the best is just about to come to you. Wait for your turn.**

Too many of us are always in a hurry to achieve what we have set out to. Let God work for you. He will give you your desire at the right time and in the right amount. After every failure, you still have another chance to try again. Actually, it is failure which steers you towards the path of success in life.

"Success consists of going from failure to failure without loss of enthusiasm."

— Winston Churchill

Yes, failure is actually a part of your success, not it's opposite. There are so many lessons to be learnt from each of your failure.

Chapter 12

CONTENTMENT

"They are truly poor who desire all, they are truly rich who desire nothing." I remember this quotation engraved on a decoration piece my father brought all the way from Delhi and nicely placed it near the phone! We all used to read it at least twice daily whenever we passed by or came to pick up a phone call. Bringing up four children must not have been easy but I have always seen my parents happy and contented.

What is Meant by Contentment?

Does contentment mean we don't have to be ambitious? Oh no! It only means that you should be happy with whatever you have *now, in this present moment.* Then, in this happy state, you can try to achieve greater heights in business, your profession, work and studies. **Your happiness should not be a contingent expression** — "I will be happy *only after* I become the General Manager of this company". Because, in such a case, your happiness will always be a 'thing of the future', something which will happen only in the future, something forthcoming.

"It isn't what you have or who you are or where you are or what you are doing that makes you happy or unhappy. It is what you think about it."

— Dale Carnegie

We keep waiting to actually start living. A contented person will always be happy. But the question arises — can there be a contented person at all? Some are after money, some are after degrees, some buy any number of houses and some buy ornaments and gold. Or, is it true that poor people are more contented than the rich? We can be contented in one realm of our life and discontented in another.

Contentment Brings Happiness in Life

Contentment in life depends on how we perceive our life situations and what kind of thoughts we have about others and ourselves. **We, not our circumstances, create our misery.**

By being contented, you are at peace with yourself. You do not wait for the approval of others and are happy from within, although you may be working hard to improve your life. The little things of life are sources of happiness for a contented person.

I am in awe of my cousin sister who works in the office in a senior position which keeps her very busy and on the move. However, she's fully aware of all the beautiful miracles of nature — beautiful flowers and trees, music, nice and inspiring quotations and lovely paintings which she keeps posting on Facebook. Facebook has become interesting for me just because of her! I appreciate her for her awareness and can make out what a contented person she must be to love so many beautiful little things.

You have heard the story of King Midas who was blessed by a hermit one day and could touch and change anything into gold. He was happy as his kingdom would become the richest. But when his food and daughter too changed into gold, he ran crying for help. He would rather bask in the sound of laughter of his dear daughter than have gold! His wish was granted, at last and he got back his happy life.

Be Satisfied With Your Own Achievements

Speaking about material possessions, how much is enough? We can become rich by decreasing our wants.

Contentment also means being satisfied with what life has given to you *now* and whatever has come your way in the *past*. I have seen a friend showing dissatisfaction openly, right in front of his old mother, remembering his poor school and teachers. Imagine a mother's predicament at that moment! He went on vocally criticizing his school teachers and how he had loathed going to his school. Wonder of wonders, his colleague has attended the same school and cherishes fond memories!

Parents try to give their best to their children with the resources at hand. You can yourself aspire to become better and bigger in life, without making them feel small or blaming them for not providing the various comforts of life you have now. **Be grateful to your parents for giving you the *life* that you are living today.**

A contented person experiences such joy that can't be experienced by outside material pleasures. He is at peace with himself. Such a person not only appreciates you for what you possess but is also happy with whatever he has, wherever he is. He is miles away from comparison. If you do not have something and you criticize the person who possesses it, you are not contented. For instance, "What is the use of your wearing such costly clothes when I myself have never ever bought any dress for more than 300 rupees?"

Well, this is not the hallmark of a contented person. On the other hand, if you say, "I am so happy that you are learning painting. As a child I did not learn this art but I am happy for you!". Yes, thus spoke a contented person.

Aspire, But Do Not Complain

But contentment is not an instrument to make you curb desire or stop dreaming. It should be made a 'way of life' to keep happy. And happiness is what we all want in our lives. Doesn't contentment come with currency and comfort? After all, there is difference between travelling in a plane and a train. The idea is to stop comparing as there will always be someone possessing more than us.

Aspire and dream for tomorrow but do not complain today. Contentment in this sense means to be grateful for where you are *now* and what you have achieved *till date.* What is the point in cribbing about what you could not do or what needs to be done tomorrow? Choose to be happy and contented now.

My friend keeps asking me about how badly he wants a change of place. He intends to be happy and work hard in the *new place.* And he has been repeating this to me for the past 15 years!

The grass always looks greener on the other side. If we evolve to be a happy person, that is what we will attract. People will become more helpful, caring and happy all around us, in turn making our life better.

Look at a tree. Just by blooming where it is planted, it grows from a tiny seed to a big tree, giving shade to passers-by, sharing its fruits, wood and the fragrance of its flowers all around its surroundings.

We should find happiness and contentment from the fact that God loves each one of us, He sends flowers to us daily, the lovely shining sun greets us and reminds us to smile and the laughter of children renews our trust in living happily.

The hug of a loving mother reveals how safe you are anywhere in this universe and the chirping birds remind us to hum our favourite song no matter how tough the going may get. The breeze and the trees... There is so much to feel contented for.

Contentment is the Key to a Happy Life

If only money gave contentment and happiness, all the rich people would be seen laughing their hearts out. Money is important for leading a comfortable life. However, it should not become the sole driving force for doing something. You must derive happiness from your work and bring in excellence in your job at hand. Money and happiness will follow!

There can be no contentment in the outside world. Only when we delve inwards, can we experience our true intrinsic nature. This is also the realm from where happiness originates.

Contentment lies in sharing with those around you, loving others, doing something that satisfies your soul, enjoying good health and a happy family life while also working hard to reach higher goals in life. However, we should not forget to enjoy our journey while striving hard to reach our destination. Some people worry so much about succeeding and reaching their goals that they forget to live in the present moment and fail to count their blessings at hand!

Contentment implies that first you must be happy with what you already have while striving to reach greater heights in terms of career, material success, etc. Decide to be happy with what you have. **Never let the things you want make you forget the things you have!** Your success in life is also defined by how contented you are.

Chapter 13

INVEST IN YOURSELF

God knew that mankind would discover and reach almost every place in this world, even the far away planets and stars in the space. So, He hid the real gems of peace, happiness, contentment and the pleasure of silence within us! He knew well that in our pursuit to discover outer realms of this universe, we will seldom go within ourselves!

But if we become aware of this now, we can still learn about a beautiful side of our life which we have missed so far. Material wealth is very necessary for our sustenance in this world but if we take care of the spiritual aspect too, we can live peacefully and happily. Such knowledge protects us from excesses of any kind and we lead a balanced and disciplined life. We are open to new knowledge of living our life in a better way and keep improving ourselves and thereby our life conditions. We are also better equipped to deal with any upheavals in our life. Vices like fear, jealousy, anger, greed stay away from us and we bask in the glory of God's love.

We book tickets to faraway places for taking a break and rejuvenate ourselves. Let us invest a few minutes and sit in silence and take a journey inwards. We will be able to slow down the whirlwind of our thoughts.

We long for the company of our friends but seldom sit in our own company.

Tackling Boredom in Life

When my friend's husband goes on tour, she feels very lonely. On the contrary, when my kids are in school and my husband goes to work in the hospital, I relish reading my favourite book in silence, sing and cook, pray in silence and seem to enjoy my own company.

Most of my books have been written during this time. I pick up phone calls and receive anyone gladly because I am in peace. I know that a lot of people complain of boredom. They pass their time somehow, watching T.V. or going off to sleep.

We all should find a higher purpose in life. We should utilize our time to grow strong spiritually, financially and physically. Spirituality also bestows us with mental strength. Where our knowledge acquired from books teaches us to see logic, our spiritual knowledge makes us comprehend miracles in our life, in nature and makes us live with *awareness*. We start rejoicing in the little pleasures of life.

One evening, when my little daughter was practicing her prayer song at home, with my husband accompanying her on the harmonium, the sweet angelic voice of a little child seemed to me like a heavenly experience. No material wealth, not even diamonds, could have given me such profound happiness at that moment of time. Similarly, the awareness of our kids around us fills our heart with love for them and gratitude to God that He chose us as their caretakers.

Finding Joy in Little Things

The evening when my 11 year old daughter prepared her first *dosa* especially for me, the afternoon when my daughter showed me her test marks 10/10 in Geography (both of us had slogged the previous night to study and learn well) or when I taught my elder daughter how to speak in a better way for an elocution are all moments which make me wealthy emotionally. This love and care has an impact on the child's health, well-being and sense of security and makes us satisfied and happy individuals too.

Upgrade Your Skills and Qualifications

Take care to educate yourself. It makes us confident individuals and upgrades our knowledge.
A woman having two kids was on stage with her husband on the occasion of 'Husband's Night' programme in a Company's colony. When her chance came to answer a few general questions on her married life, she spoke in broken English (to everyone's amusement) and even used 'she' while referring to her husband! Everyone in the audience found this funny and had a hearty laugh. She was the talk of the colony for the entire week. **Where the story ended for others, it actually began for her.**

She got enrolled in a graduation course taking English Language as the main subject. She had to travel 30 kilometres from the colony by the Company van along with school kids whenever she had to attend college in the nearby town. This went on for some years and by the time all the ladies in the neighbourhood became aware about what she was doing, she had completed her Ph.D. in English! She was also later invited to plan and write for the Company's bimonthly magazine! She invested in herself and utilized her time by working hard.

When my kids were very young, I too studied Law, came back home before my daughters' school was over, cooked the meals and was ready to receive them. But I was a happier person as I experienced a sense of achievement. I finished Master of Human Rights by correspondence. Our family travelled all the way to Delhi so that I could attend contact classes.

"The swiftest way to triple your success is to double your investment in personal development."
— Robin Sharma

Later in life, I felt that I had to learn programming otherwise I would have to depend on others for simple tasks. I got admission in M.Sc (I.T.) and completed it with very good grades. Since then, I have written hundreds of blogs and Web content for IT companies apart from writing manuscript for my books.

I became an alchemist digging diamonds lying within myself, sitting in peace everyday and writing for so many other brothers and sisters around the world. I enjoyed writing as this knowledge would benefit others and along this journey, I discovered my own vocation too.
I figured out that this is what I would like to do the rest of my life — spread love, solace and peace to souls who needed it most all around the world. I respect myself for such an investment and am thankful to my family, friends and teachers for extending support throughout.

Take Care of Your Mind and Body

Investing in yourself includes that you work on your emotions: anger, jealousy, hate and restlessness. You should embrace peace, read good books, pray, have love for everyone, stay away from negative words in your conversations and forgive all those who have ever hurt you. Pray for them instead.

Investing in yourself at the basic level means to take care of your body: taking a bath daily, wearing properly-fitted clothes and being well-dressed throughout the day; going for regular check-ups, having eight glasses of water daily, eating every meal at the proper time including adequate intake of juice and fruits. When you decide to eat outside food, choose a neat and nice place to dine. **You are as good as you think yourself to be. By going to best places, you will attract best of people and places for yourself.**

Investing in yourself means to take care that your friends and relatives are alright, giving time to your children's studies and showing enthusiasm when they participate in sports and cultural activities.

Your house should be well kept, with pots of green plants and all the articles should be found in their proper places. Pray to God every morning and be careful of what kind of inputs you are receiving for your mind. Your thoughts throughout the day will depend on these inputs and will accordingly generate negative or positive thoughts.
Yes, improvement begins with YOU. Learn something new every day and keep upgrading yourself. You must move with the times. Upgrade your knowledge and skills continuously.

Evaluate Yourself Rather Than Changing Others

In case you want a change, change yourself. **Don't waste precious energy going out and telling others to mend themselves so that YOU feel alright.** Instead, change yourself into a more peace-loving individual. Be humble, compassionate and treat the poor and needy with respect.

Investing in yourself includes that you sit down prayerfully, close your eyes and thank God for all that He has given you. Be in gratitude and enjoy what has been given to you by the Almighty. I witnessed a miracle when I saw a new born baby, and felt as if it is a signature of God to define His presence.

Keep Learning New Skills

One day my brother-in-law suddenly felt so sick and weak that he was even unable to walk. My sister panicked in the middle of the night and somehow they managed to sit in the car. But who would drive the car? My sister had a license but had not driven the car for months together. Now she was so nervous that she would not be able to drive at all.

So, my brother-in-law took to the steering wheel and drove to and fro and somehow, as the road was not very crowded, they reached the hospital and my brother-in-law got admitted. That night was an eye opener for my sister. In the next few weeks, she learnt to drive and practiced driving the car every day.

"An investment in knowledge always pays the best interest"
— Benjamin Franklin

Today, my sister has a separate car for herself and teaches in a reputed school. She drives all the way to her workplace. She took a lesson and invested in herself.

It is very sad to see people occupying high posts in offices who have become too fat and flabby. Gaining in one field does not necessarily mean that you have to lose in the other. Weight gain makes you walk slowly and also has impact on your self-esteem. It is a precursor of various ailments too. We must take care of our personality and overall disposition and make improvements if required.

We should be *aware* of ourselves and our surroundings. When we eat, we must be aware of what is going inside our body. Is it necessary to eat that much? Some people have acidity and still they do not have the will-power to stop drinking tea and coffee.
Similarly, we should take a break every one hour while working on the computer. Otherwise, we will suffer from problems relating to our neck, backbone and eye sight. Here too, self-control is needed. So stop, rest and start working again after sometime for your own good.

All these are investments which make our body vibrant. We can thus work hard for many more years in future. **Make it a point to invest in yourself and see your professional, personal and financial life bloom.**

Time to put your best self forward!

Chapter 14

VALUE RELATIONSHIPS

Relationships are all about bonds of love that we share with those we trust and care for. These relationships make us smile, stand beside us when we cry, care and share love and affection and make us laugh freely without fear or inhibitions. They accept us as we are.

Relationships Bring Love in Life

Our relationships give us the daily doses of love that our body and soul require for living a healthy life. Immanuel Kant has commented on rules for happiness—

> ***"Something to do,***
> ***Someone to love,***
> ***Something to hope for."***

The daily phone call that connects me to my mother, fills me with zest for life and I come running to pick up the phone from anywhere inside the house or even downstairs. It brings for me such love which nothing else in the world can compare or fill up.

What is one common thing every one craves for? It is love. Such a simple word yet so many are longing for it every day. **Love others for what they are, how they are, not for what *you* want them to be.** Love others unconditionally, honestly and truthfully. When you fill your being with love, you make yourself healthier and happier.

My 12-year-old daughter is very fond of lipstick and she got a chance to put her favourite pink colour for the Teacher's Day celebration in her school. Once she put the lipstick as I do, she wanted pink rosy cheeks too! My daughter handed over the lipstick to me and asked me to apply the pink shade with my fingers on her cheeks. I told her it could harm her skin, but she was not ready to listen. Kids want to do everything mamma does! So, I thought of another way—and put lipstick on one finger but rubbed another one on her face.

While I was doing this, my daughter's happiness knew no bounds! Then she went to the mirror and was surprised to find not a shade of pink on her cheek! "Hey, what's this," she exclaimed. Both of us had a hearty laugh. My daughter understood that I meant to care for her and went to school without complaining.

Yet another time, my younger daughter wanted to buy a light blue dress only because I too have a dress of the same colour. She delighted in the fact that we would both wear similar dresses together. Such mutual love and feeling of warmth is heavenly.

A great relationship is about two things: First find out the similarities and second, respect the differences.

When I told my elder sister that I would buy a tablet, her whole family came on the phone one by one, discussing which one is right for me, and the latest one in the market with better features, etc. The mobile actually became more than just a thing. It brought the whole family together under one roof for a thorough discussion and after my husband bought it for me, everyone rejoiced congratulating me asking me for my mobile number even before it was activated!

A surprise SMS just to show that you remember someone is enough to make them happy. It shows that you thought about that person.

"A true relationship is having someone who accepts your past, supports your present, loves you and encourages your future."

— Anonymous

I love to receive informative e-mails from my uncle. If I do not receive any e-mail from him for a week, I send him one. What he does is just forward the nice e-mails to all his contacts. His e-mails have made me wiser, no doubt. They are about how to take care of your health, about spirituality, newly formulated laws with some being humorous too. I am grateful to him for sending these e-mails to me.

Valuing relationships includes being in gratitude for everyone who touches our life each day and makes our journey of life joyful. This may include our friends, neighbours, colleagues and even our house maid who helps to keep our house neat and clean.

Relationships are Built on Foundation of Love

Every relationship is built on the foundation of love, respect and mutual concern. Our relationships with people in our neighbourhood should be cordial. We should enquire about the well-being of our friends at times, reach out to help them at the time of need and treat them with respect. They become our extended family wherever we live.

One of the best gifts you can give someone is thanking them for being part of your life.

Our neighbour's daughter rushed to our house one Sunday morning crying aloud for help. It randomly occurred to me that she must have got scared of a dog. But how could I go to help her as I was more afraid of a dog than anyone else I ever knew! But then, her father came rushing and panting saying that his son had fainted all of a sudden. For the past half an hour his son was restless, speaking incoherently.

All the neighbours got together and without even waiting for the hospital ambulance, put him on a blanket. This 17-year-old boy was very heavy to lift up but we all were there to help and did not lose hope. We put him down on the ground for a few seconds to take rest and picked him up again till we finally reached the car. The boy reached hospital in time and was admitted in the Intensive Care Unit.

After 15 days of loving care and medication, he became alright. Today, when I see him running on the passage that leads to our house, the scene when he looked totally lifeless comes across my mind. I feel proud that we were all there to help him.

"Generally speaking, the most miserable people I know are those who are obsessed with themselves; the happiest people I know are those who lose themselves in the service of others... by and large, I have come to see that if we complain about life, it is because we are thinking only of ourselves."

— Gordon B. Hinckley

People living close to us are our relatives first because they will be the ones to help us when we need help. Everyone else will take time to arrive from other cities. We must value all of them like we value gems. They won't be perfect people, nonetheless we should make it a habit to focus on the positive side and ignore the negative qualities, we should never involve ourselves in any brawl, never speak ill of anyone and never take sides. **We should be able to boast of our entire neighbourhood as our friend.**

In a beautiful and fulfilling relationship, it matters that there is flow of love between people. **Any negative thought will give rise to negative vibrations which tend to reach an individual even before you open your mouth! So, entertain positive thoughts about individuals you want to build relations with.**

Give time to people from your own schedule, keep promises, show respect and concern and be with people you love when they are going through difficult times.

I personally feel so happy that my daughter Sangeet and I went to meet my mother and brother, albeit for a day, all the way from Jamshedpur to Bengaluru, when my mother underwent her Pacemaker operation.

I could experience their happiness on seeing us. There was so much positive energy around and the most important message we delivered to them was that 'We care for you and love you.'

I read these beautiful lines some time back:

Relationship is not just a word
Not merely a friendship
It's a silent commitment
which says, I'll be with you.

There is another one I must mention here:
Relation and medicine play same role in our life. Both care for us in pain... The only difference is that a relationship has no expiry date.

Loving in Good and Bad Times

When we speak of relationships, it also means loving the other person when he is weak and ill. If relationship means to enjoy together, it also means to care for the other when he needs your help. Our family friend Mr. Singh used to tell us, "Don't visit your friend during celebrations and birthday parties if you are hard pressed of time. But never, ever miss out going to visit a sick person or attending a funeral." If you contemplate, you will find that the people you love the most are those who stood by you during challenging times. You will still remember the touch of their hand on your shoulder conveying to you that everything will be alright.

It's not about 'I', 'my', it is about 'we' and 'our'.

Breathing Life into Your Relationships

During tough times, the bond of love must be present without any trace of anger. Illness can come to anyone, anytime. **If you are fine and can be of help to someone, don't wait a second to reach out to your friend, neighbour or relative. Now is the test of your relationship.** Now is the time to strengthen the bond of love and breathe life into it. Care, love, share, give, protect and do whatever it takes to heal the other person. By taking care of the 'other' person, you are actually taking care of yourself. You are building a strong character and a good health by positive feelings of compassion, love, trust and help.

A true loving relationship is about trust. It is not possessive, instead it gives freedom. It allows you to be *you* — as you are, without any need to change for someone else. You do not have to pretend about anything in a loving relationship.

Love cares and shows that you are special. When I was in school, our neighbour used to keep really busy in the office. Once, while he was talking to us and enquiring about our classes, he wrongly mentioned his son's class. When we corrected him, he said that he kept so busy that he never realized that his much older son had come to senior school! We really found it too hilarious and surprising to believe this. I believe that working hard doesn't mean that you ignore those for whom you are working day and night!

There is another person we know who never applied for a holiday when his son was born and even kept busy with work when the family was celebrating his first birthday. He is never around at home during any of the festivals and yes, to top it all, has missed important occasions such as when his son appeared for his Board Exams or when his old father remembered him and wanted to meet him when he was bedridden— all in the name of being busy at work. He does not realize that he has actually missed out on landmark events of his life which will never come back again.

Know this—Balance your work and personal life. What is the use of regretting later? You will never, ever get the special moments of your life back again. Will you ever be totally free from work? Never!

"Love is that condition in which the happiness of another person is essential to your own."
— Robert A. Heinlein

You have to find time amidst your demanding and hectic schedule. This is also what defines to your near and dear ones how much you love them and care for them.

Relationship with Yourself!

When we talk of relationships, this also includes relationship with yourself. To understand yourself, your passion, your desire in life, be happy and peaceful and take care of yourself both physically and mentally. Respect yourself and only then others will respect you. Eat and sleep well, be well-dressed, upgrade your skills, be well-informed, courteous to others and keep a peaceful countenance. Negative conversations, bitching, cribbing and arguments are not for you. Well, with such a disciplined life, success beckons you at every step!

An acquaintance, a very old man, did not have a hearing aid which he was trying to procure from one of the medical camps held from time to time. So, whenever he visited us, he did the talking and I just listened. I only made gestures when I wanted to ask him if he wanted tea.
Once, he opened up about his family and it was quite sad to learn that his daughter-in-law often asked him to leave their house in frustration.

We had always appreciated the fact that he kept so cheerful and prayerful. His eyes always had this glint of happiness when he spoke about God and his younger days.
So one day, I coaxed my husband to buy him the hearing aid at our personal expense and help him. My husband answered in the affirmative but also added something very profound. He said that this man was happy because he is not able to hear properly. His inputs are what he reads (spiritual magazines) and devotional songs. If he will start hearing what his son and his son's wife crib about and curse him all day long, his happiness will be gone and his freedom will be lost!
I really thought that my husband was right. But **in life, we have to learn to be happy in spite of certain people or situations that we do not like.** So, the real test of happiness for this man would start after he wore his hearing aid!

For leading a happy life, we have to banish jealousy, fear, guilt and anger from our lives. **Filter the incidents and make them a residue to get the filtrate of happiness.** These beautiful lines sum up what love in a true relationship should really mean:

"Love knows no limits to its endurance, no end to its trust, no fading of its hope; it can outlast anything. It is in fact, the only thing that stands when all else has fallen."

— Elizabeth Elliot

What Does Happiness Bring for YOU?

Happiness brings peace, calm and tranquillity. **When we are happy, our creative energies are fanned and we are able to tap our inner potential.** It requires least energy to do so and keeps us perpetually in an altogether different plane.

We feel free and light.

There are no surplus negative thoughts passing through our mind.

We remain prayerful and in gratitude.

We become *aware* and live in the present moment.

We are in awe of nature and its beauty and live each moment in joy.

We experience bliss and exude warmth and love.

We are also more caring, sharing and compassionate with our fellow beings because what is in our inside, we will exude on our outside.

Our thoughts stop wandering in the past clutter or in the future fears.

We are filled with positive energy and are charged to work harder.

Earlier, we were in emotional pain, worked hard in the outside world and became tired fast. Stress went hand in hand and we wondered why happiness eluded us. But now, we do all our work in joy, without worry, without trying to change other people or molding them according to what we think is right.

Actually, we 'let go' and in turn assist ourselves in reaching the highest rung of success — walking our way up the ladder of success peacefully and happily. **Now, the outside circumstances don't control our inner emotions. We unlock our own inherent power.**

"Where ever you go, no matter what the weather, always bring your own sunshine."
— Anthony J.D' Angelo

Happiness is the only way to lead a meaningful life. *Filtering* also means not to give too much attention to negative incidents. Ignore them and don't repeat them aloud to others or even to yourself in your mind space.
I read a murder mystery in the newspaper —a really negative story which did have some impact on my mind. In the afternoon, I wanted to relate the whole story to my husband, when he came home for lunch. However, I stopped myself. Then, I was inclined to discuss this story with my mother while talking to her on phone, but I decided, again, to filter the incident.

Why should I relate a story which will trigger a series of negative conversations or negative thoughts throughout the day? Instead, I took up inspiring stories and discussed about some nice books I had come across in the library that day. Both my husband and mother looked energized after conversing with me.

Who knows, they must have discussed this with their friends in the evening. **So, it made me happy that what I gave was a filtrate of happiness. The negative stories were held back like residue.**

We should avoid repetition of negative incidents and people whom we come across throughout the day. Whenever my daughters relate negative incidents from their school — their teacher scolded them, they got late to school, had a quarrel with their classmate etc., we listen to them the first time. However, we put a warning tag asking them not to repeat those incidents again in front of someone or think about them again and again. This is because these incidents would inflict similar pain in their minds all over again. So, we pretend to press the *delete* button— which is actually their pug little nose!

"What lies behind us and what lies before us are tiny matters compared to what lies within us."
— Ralph Waldo Emerson

Two sisters living in the same city were suddenly not in talking terms with each other.

"Why did you not give me your address before moving to your new house?" complained one.

"Why did you not come to see us off when you knew the exact date we were shifting?" argued the other.

There were any number of complaints and they did not talk to each other for a year! However, *Rakshabandhan* was round the corner. *Rakshabandhan* is a festival in India which celebrates the loving relationship between brothers and sisters.

"Oh, I will send the *rakhees*, but I won't patch up," said one.
"Who cares," said the other.

The daughter of one of the sisters was supposed to tie *rakhee* on the arms of her cousin brother. Her cousin became adamant that he would meet and greet his little sister and personally get the *rakhee* tied by her on his wrist. What a predicament!

Both the sisters had to relent now and so talked over the phone to decide the programme for the *Rakshabandhan* festival. The elder sister arrived with goodies and sweets and congratulated her sister for the new house. The younger sister prepared a nice lunch and they had a joyous festival!
Looks so easy now. But it took them nearly a year to smile at each other again! It took the efforts of their young kids to bring two ladies in their 40's together!

In another incident, a full-time caretaker forgets to keep the tiffin box of the child in the school bag. When the mother (who was a teacher) reaches school, she discovers this and her anger knows no bounds. She calls the caretaker on phone to convey angrily that since she has committed the mistake, she has to rectify! She should either come all the way to school in the private bus or she should hand the tiffin to the bus driver of the school bus. The caretaker manages the latter after some running about and had a hectic day. Could this situation be solved in an easier way? Of course! The mother could have bought chips and cakes from the school shop and asked her daughter to enjoy a picnic that day.

You have to acknowledge that people working for you won't be perfect all the time. You have to keep space for little misgivings. You can make mistakes too! Treat others as you would like to be treated. If you do not have the patience to stand by others during times of need, you too will find yourself standing alone when you need help most. What you give returns back to you. Give love, respect and happiness to enjoy the same!

"To forgive is to set a prisoner free and discover that the prisoner was you."
— Lewis B. Smedes

Once, when I had just got married, I left the milk to boil and forgot about it. My husband went to the kitchen and switched off the gas. Then he went off to work. In the evening, I thanked him for helping me and not blaming me for my folly. He smiled and asked me to be more careful while dealing with gas and fire as they can be dangerous. I learnt the lesson but also felt the respect my husband had for me.

Such things pass on and then become a habit of every member in the family. Let us not catch the other person doing wrong. Instead, let us stand by the other person to find a solution together and help each other.
Fix the problem, not the person! A few days later, our neighbour handed us our house keys. She said that when

my husband had opened the main door, he had forgotten the keys on the door! Now, it was my chance to confront him— but I told him about the incident without going into a 'blaming mode'. He has been careful ever since.

All these incidents do give us some fear and stress although they may seem like everyday matters. **Just like the climate of a place depends on everyday weather of any place, our general health too depends upon the quality of daily incidents in our life.** That is the reason why you should take care of each moment today to enjoy good health tomorrow.

There are instances where siblings have not forgiven each other— even when one of them has passed away! The grievances were carried in the mind and taken to the heart so fiercely that there was no space left for forgiveness at all.

"Forgiveness does not change the past, but it does enlarge the future."
— Paul Boese

We are all self-sufficient with children, their achievements, our branded furniture, big cars and foreign trips to boast of.

What then, is eluding each one of us?

Why is our quest for happiness such an unending process?

This is because we consider ourselves separate from the other person. It should be: *He is me and she is also me. Her mistake is also my mistake. When I forgive, I forgive myself.* Love each person dearly and focus only on their positive qualities. Try to learn from them. You will be happiness personified.

Chapter 15

DON'T JUDGE OTHERS

"Hey, this old book with brown cover! What book is this lying here?" I grumbled while cleaning the house early in the morning. Looking for a corner to dump it, my eyes suddenly focused on the author's name. So, I thought I would rest for a few minutes and flip through the book.

And I went on reading, cancelling all my cleaning work and other assignments, one page after another, totally engrossed. I felt energized and filled with renewed energy and I got answers to a few questions that were going on in my mind for a couple of days. The book was later kept respectfully among my favourites!

My husband had taken it out from a box the previous night and had kept it carelessly on the chair. Imagine, I was judging the book by its cover! The whole day, we judge people, things and even our own selves, rather harshly, even without actually being aware of it.

Here is one example. Early one morning, even before I said 'hello' to my neighbour, I was initially taken aback by the large T-shirt and outsized pants she was wearing. I judged even before I myself could realize! Likewise, we keep judging throughout the day and lose the opportunity to connect lovingly with so many souls whom we can reach out with few positive and encouraging words.

Judging prevents us from looking at the goodness that lies in the other person. When we judge, we switch off the button that transmits loving vibrations from us. We do not give out love when we judge. So, to help ourselves, we need to focus only on the good qualities of others and desist from focusing on the negatives.

We must accept others for what they are and not for what they ought to be. Because then, our focus will shift to changing others rather than changing ourselves.

We must elevate our thoughts to the next level of— 'let go, non-judgment, non-criticism, prayer, compassion, love and respect' for the other person. Judging others means finding faults with them and sending negative energies to them.

Where there is no love, there cannot be any happiness inside you. When you hate the other person, the container carrying that hate is actually you. So, indirectly, you are taxing yourself mentally and physically. Forgive if you were hurt and move on.

Relationships last longer because two people made a choice to keep it, fight for it and work for it.

Press the 'delete' button in your mind and don't repeat unpleasant incidents in your mind or while talking with someone else. *Engrave* beautiful and delightful thoughts in your mind. You can care only without judging and this brings out gems like patience, tolerance and unconditional love.

Love is such a powerful emotion. It conveys to the other person that you love them in health and in sickness, in success and in failure. Their sorrows and failures become yours. **The power of love and non-judgment doesn't question, "what will I receive from the other person?" It thrives on trust and caring without expectations.**

Love and judgmental behaviour can't stay together.

Read these beautiful lines:

"Relationship is not how long you have been together, not how much you have given or received, not how many times you have helped each other; it's how you value one another."

If we judge, we will be judged too. This vicious cycle will give rise to stress in life. We not only make others uncomfortable, but spoil our own comfort too. We must 'accept the isness of what is', and enjoy this world in its natural and true flavour.

Wearing red glasses will show us only danger everywhere. It boils down to what you are focusing on in life — the good or the ugly. What we focus on also becomes a part of your personality. We can only meet happiness on the path of positive thoughts and loving actions.

What You Focus on Grows!

Craft a beautiful life by looking at the brighter side of life, by contemplating not on what sorrows life has handed to you but by focusing on what reasons you have in life to smile. Learn magnanimity from the sky, from the trees and from the flowers that spread fragrance even in the hands that crush them.

"It is impossible to experience the world as it is, while you are judging it."
— Gary Rudz

In case of unpleasant incidents and illnesses, don't accuse or hate others. Also, do not blame yourself for any mistake you made. Lead a life of prayer and be empowered rather than living a life of repentance and grief holding on to blunders of the past.

"Correcting oneself is correcting the whole world. The sun is simply bright. It does not correct anyone. Because it shines, the whole world is full of light. Transforming yourself is a means of giving light to the world."
— Ramana Maharshi

Forgive, let go, be good and keep positive. The Universe is after all a lovely place to be in and it will take care of you. It will bestow you with all the happiness that you can imagine because what you draw on the canvas of your mind, comes to picture.

Remember, you bring forth in your life what you focus on most. Make positive and happy thoughts your friends for life. You will find happiness within you!

Chapter 16

TAKING CARE OF NUTRITION

Our happiness depends on our well-being. If we are not healthy, we will show symptoms of anger, irritation and weakness. In such a condition, who can expect us to be happy? This is to say that our mental health and physical health are both interconnected. If we enjoy good health, our feel-good factor will keep us happy too. Little irritations won't bother us and fatigue, general ailments like cold and fever too will stay at bay.

In terms of nutrition, food for our body and fodder for the mind serve important purpose too. Just like it is important to take care of what fruits and vegetables we eat, how much we eat, what time we eat our meals daily, it is also important to understand and be aware of what kind of thoughts and discussions we are entertaining throughout the day.

The best of foods cannot give us good health if we watch violence on television and discuss negative issues and gossip throughout the day. This also includes raking out past forlorn packages of hurts and ego-issues and repentance for minor incidents in life.

Having fresh fruit juice (e.g. combination of apple, gourd, *amla*, carrot etc.), salads with meals, fresh fruits, coconut water and citrus fruit juice etc. will keep you in good health. Your immunity will be strong and you will have more stamina. Have at least 5-6 glasses of water daily. It will help to rehydrate your skin and keep you healthy and happy.

Prayer also forms a type of nutrition for self-confidence and keeps you free from worry. It connects you with the main Source of positive energy (the Almighty) and recharges you throughout the day. It elevates your plane of thoughts and indirectly guides you to think fruitful and useful thoughts.

Each petal in the universe whispers in our ears that an unknown power is at work. If we align ourselves with this divine energy, offer our work to Him and move on, we will never have any worries and anxieties in our life. You have a choice each precious day about how you will live your life: speak and hear ill of others or tune in to the Almighty. The latter rejuvenates and the former eats away our enthusiasm and vitality.

Nutrition includes the quality of thoughts we entertain in our minds. This energy percolates to our whole family by the way we speak, behave and react. **For a healthy lifestyle, the energy pervading our living space, should be positive.**

Food for the body is not enough. There must be food for the soul.

We know a family of four where the husband and wife do not converse with the old member at all. Their son has also become a part of this drama. A visit to their house easily suggests the presence of a sort of negative energy in their house. Where is room for any creativity then? **Where there will be love, peace, faith, cordial relationship, respect for others and genuine concern for each other, happiness will surely reside permanently in such an abode.**

Not having meals at the proper time is like saying that you want to go to market but you don't have the time to refill the petrol in your car! How far can you take such a vehicle? Also, awareness is required to understand the quantity and quality of our food intake. When we are eating, we should be 'present' and 'in the moment'. Try not to be in the past or future while eating. **Being angry while eating will mean putting in vibrations of anger inside our body which is unhealthy.**

"Food is everything. Food, friends, family: Those are the most important things in life."
— Zac Posen

Daily exercise, morning or evening walk, meditation and yoga too have impact on our general health.
My husband stopped taking his hypertension medicine from the time he started meditation every evening. Regular evening walks with friends saw him as a happier person and his weight too was under check. Consequently, he became more aware as to what he was consuming, steering away from sweets and fatty foods, watching less television and sleeping on time at night. **Discipline in one area of your life leads to discipline in other fields too.** No more of watching late night cricket matches or films on television. The best part is that he feels good about himself.

What is Meant by Good Health?

Good health means being healthy in mind, body and spirit; being one in word and in deed and enjoying peace of mind. Your conscience should be clear. Good health includes doing the right things, loving everyone, being contented and rising above petty issues and indulgences; rising above fear, jealousy, hatred, laziness and procrastination.

Just as we charge our phone for it to function well, we should take care of our body and mind to lead a happy and fulfilling life. Sleep is a very important factor to lead a happy life. If you are well rested, your immunity level will be much higher, your body will be healed, leaving you energized and fresh.

There is enough time for all of us to work and also take rest, if we do not stand in between our work to chat on phone or gossip standing in a group. That doesn't mean being mechanical; greet your colleagues while at work but keep a watch on yourself to check if you are wasting precious time in frivolous talks.

Complaining about your organization too won't serve any purpose. Your boss will remain the same, your place will remain the same; only you will become a habitual complainer! **Either do something about what you detest in your life otherwise accept it and carry on lovingly and happily.**

Our whole life is wasted in trying to change others. **For a change, try to change yourself! It is easier and at least under your control.** Changing oneself will include basic rules of good living like letting go, forgiveness, positive thinking, peacefulness of mind, being prayerful and being honest to yourself and to others.

Let go negative thoughts. Do not constantly crib about people who do not make you feel good about yourself. **Make happiness a priority in your life. Be aware of your own emotions throughout the day.** Ignore negative thoughts or replace them with some other positive thought e.g. when you won a prize, or your birthday celebration when you had fun with your loved ones together. Pick up memories of something from your life for which you can be grateful and glad. Thank God for your eyes, your sweet voice, doting parents or good friends etc.

Whatever profession we choose, where ever we live, whatever we do throughout the day for ourselves and for others, our prime purpose is to be happy. Actually, the very purpose of our life on this planet is to be fulfilled, happy and contented. So, be happy now!

Chapter 17

LISTENING TO MUSIC

Talking about music, let me begin from the very beginning. Our heart beat, the beautiful music of the cool blowing wind, the waterfalls and chirping birds are some of the musical sounds nature has bestowed on us.

Live with such awareness that you are able to hear the peaceful sounds of nature. Feel your own breath. The hustle and bustle, hurry and noise all around us fills us with anxiety and stress. But in nature, everything unfolds at the proper time, silently.

Silence is the language of nature. That is why meditation fills us with peace. There is no noise when the little seed sprouts to become a mighty tree one day. So, become more *alive* to the sounds of nature. In our day to day life, we don't even give heed to these things, which are God's little valuable gifts to us. **Nature and music are direct roads that lead you to God — the Creator.**

"Music washes away from the soul, the dust of everyday life."
— Berthold Auerbach

How true! I remember the first time I heard the sound of the strings of a violin in a Radio Station in Delhi, the beautiful sound of the instrument touched the core of my being; I was instantly taken to some other realm at that moment. It connected me to myself; to my very being or to the Almighty, I cannot say. But the impact that its sound had on my soul was inexplicable.

Music brings peace. It reaches your soul to give you solace. It lets you forget the worries of your life and elevates your soul to an altogether different level of existence. *Music relaxes you and fills you with love and prayer.*

Music can instil hope and courage too. It is a universal language. Words are not so important as is the flow of various musical notes that carry you to another world where there are no fears, frustrations, worries and anxieties. Music brings to the forefront our emotions, and emotions are common all over the world irrespective of caste, creed, race, skin colour or nationality.

During my pregnancy, I used to listen to soothing *ghazals* (a type of music) sung by Indian singer Jagjit Singh and did not feel nausea throughout the day. I did not feel alone and bored after my husband went to work. The soothing songs were like balm to my ears and put me to sleep.

I remember a few moments in my life when I was so engrossed in music to even be aware of what was happening around me. I recall one instance when I was standing in the kitchen boiling milk. Just then I remembered my favourite song and I started correcting the nuances all on my own, singing aloud, at a high pitch. I was looking towards the ceiling in order to touch the right notes. The milk overflowed out of the container into the kitchen drain — all this in my very presence!

In yet another incident, I missed my bus stop and reached the main bus depot, had to take another bus back home and spent the entire day travelling! I was engrossed in practicing the new classical *raaga* with my eyes closed and was totally immersed in music.

Well, life in itself is a song; sing aloud as if no one is listening. "The woods would be dark and lonely if only those birds sang that sang the best." Or better still, sing as if you are singing for God.

Here is a story my friend narrated to me some time back. Tansen was a great singer in King Akbar's court and was considered to be one of his 'court jewels'. One morning, Akbar heard someone singing beautifully. He inquired about this unknown voice from Birbal, his Court Minister. Birbal always knew the answer.
He told the king that this song is more beautiful than words can explain because while Tansen sings in praise of you and to please you, the king— this man is singing for God. This explains the added beauty in his songs. This other singer was none other than Baiju Bawra.

Music is also another word for meditation. It incorporates breathing exercises. It involves all prayers and is therefore a source of joy in life. **Music is the language of the soul.** For a happy life, make this vehicle a part of your life. It inspires in so many ways and gives happiness. Without it, life would be drab and boring.

We have lot of drums and music in all festivals to dance and enjoy. It is really impossible to imagine this world without its sweet sounds and rhythms. Even listening to music brings positive vibrations in your house. Good, soothing music connects you with the Divine, thereby bringing peace of mind.

Music has therapeutic effect on the soul. It increases concentration and one learns to sit at one place peacefully, without any disturbance or rushing here and there doing umpteen chores. It helps overcome depression and makes an individual confident and disciplined. Singing or learning to play a musical instrument needs practice and dedication. You have to sit and practice for long hours before you play a piece correctly. Music gives you patience and this discipline percolates and defines itself in other areas of your life as well.

I made my daughter Anandita learn the first 20 elements of the Periodic Table in Chemistry by singing the names of the elements to a specific tune. This is also how she had learnt, as a toddler, the days of the week and months of the year! We sang them together and the lesson was done in a few minutes!

Music is effective in treating ailments too. For instance, *raag bhupali, raag todi* and *raag ahir bhairav* are said to provide relief from cold, headache and high blood pressure. *Raag bhairvi* is believed to provide relief from sinus, cold and phlegm. *Raag malkauns* and *raag asavari* can help you do away with your age old low blood pressure problem and *raag chandrakauns* can help in the treatment of heart ailments and diabetes.

Each *raaga* is best sung at a specific time of the day. For example, *raag yaman* is sung in the evening and *raag bhairav* is sung in the morning. Each musical note has been derived from nature, e.g. *pancham* is said to have been derived from the nightingale's voice. *Raagas* also depict specific moods and seasons. *Raag Megh malhar* depicts rainy season with the specific combination of notes used in this *raaga*.

"The greater part of our happiness or misery depends upon our dispositions, and not upon our circumstances."
— Martha Washington

Like the *raagas* in music, our life should be tuned to happiness, no matter what season of life we are going through. It can't rain forever; so if you are going through a rough patch in our life, be certain that the rainbow of happiness will shine in your life soon.

During my trip to Bengaluru, I felt that most of the trip comprised of us being driven by pilot, bus driver, cab driver, train driver etc.! The pilot steered the plane through the clouds and shining sunlight, the cab driver drove in the dark of the night, sometimes also through broken and water clogged roads. The train driver towed us all through dense tunnels, bridges, cultivated fields and forests. Hey, I thought, this is indeed what life is composed of! If we become the drivers of our life, we must patiently yet surely drive through good and bad times and arrive safely at our destination. In between, pray a little, hum a little and have patience and faith in yourself and in the Almighty.

Keep your patience and let the clouds pass by. **Wait and win! Be happy, not hapless!** Smile, for it will bring forth brightness and happiness in your life.

Chapter 18

JOY OF GIVING

God gives and forgives; Man gets and forgets. God is so fond of giving that even after he gave us sweet water inside the coconut, he was not too satisfied and went on to give a little more. He filled it up with some coconut for us to eat lest we feel hungry.

God gave me eyes, ears, legs and good health and I am always in gratitude for His gifts to me. However, He did not stop here. He gave the gift of a sweet and melodious voice too so that I would never get bored in my life! It is a gift to be carried further through me. I can entertain and make people happy whenever I get a chance.

God's love for us is evident from the colourful fruits and vegetables, fragrances and flavours that He created for all of us. We too should make it a point to pass on happiness, compassion, smile, gratitude, peace and love to others who come in contact with us throughout the day.
Even when we are faced with problems in our life, God is already aware that we do have the inner grit within us to overcome fear and solve it. We have to keep our faith in ourselves and in God.

The more we share, the more we have!

Giving Brings Joy

This applies not only in the realm of giving gifts and presents, it actually applies more to sincerity and love that you pour in while giving. Case in point: a sincere compliment.

I was quite tired after the third round during my morning walk, when I met an acquaintance. The couple was out early morning as the wife was learning how to drive a car. The husband complimented me saying I was looking like a 20-year-old! Believe me, all said and done, no philosophy applied, I felt rejuvenated then and there. I felt good. Henceforth, I have never missed going for my early morning walk! **Beautiful words, sincerely spoken can be the best gifts one can give.**

My grandmother always tutored us to keep 1% of our monthly earnings separately for giving it as charity to the needy, at a wedding or in any religious place of worship. She believed that this would augment our earnings while giving us satisfaction of having helped those in need.

It is true that what we give to others, we give to ourselves.

Mrs. Radon used to invite young girls playing in the ground near her house. When they showed up at her house, she offered them water in her most beautiful glasses. Then she opened her box which contained colourful necklaces made from very good quality big and small beads, and handed out one necklace to every girl in the group. The girls rushed out really happy, back to the field to resume playing.

She was just another middle-aged woman who loved kids, we thought. The necklaces in my own collection kept multiplying too — most of them gifted by her. Mrs. Radon herself did not come out of her house very often.

One day, my mother happened to meet her and as she was the only American lady in our colony, my mother recognized her. She knew that this was the lady we talked about and praised most of our evenings.

"Thanks for your lovely necklaces. Allow me to ask why you give them to all these little girls?" enquired my mother.

"Well," she replied, "I too had my own pretty angel and had she been alive, she would be of their age. She was very fond of necklaces and had a huge collection. I feel happy interacting with the girls and experience great joy in giving them the necklaces."

Today, after 35 years, even my own kids know who Mrs. Radon was because every necklace that I buy today for myself or for my kids, reminds me of her.

Giving may not necessarily include material things. A warm smile or a sincere compliment, a few words of wisdom or beautiful loving remarks spoken from the heart are all means of giving, which the other person remembers forever. **Giving, sharing, showing kindness and mercy fill your bank of love and you are blessed with a happy life.**

"No one has ever become poor by giving."

— Anne Frank

A ray of hope you gave to someone through your words or a gentle pat on your shoulder when someone said that things would be alright, are gifts you cannot measure in terms of money.

What Should you Give to Others?

Sheba has a habit of picking up a fruit from the fruit basket placed on the dining table and handing away an apple, orange or packet of biscuits to employees who come to fix the tap, pick up the garbage or even electricians. She feels that they keep going all around for work and must be hungry. Her hands pass away food to others and she feels an inner joy by giving.
Just read these beautiful lines about what you can give others—

To your enemy, forgiveness;
to an opponent, tolerance;
to a friend, your heart;
to a customer, service;
to all, charity;
to every child, a good example
and to yourself, respect.

— Oren Arnold

My friend has a hobby of making PowerPoint Presentations and then email them to all her friends. These cover spiritual or health related topics. It is such a good feeling to read words of wisdom, hope, love and prayer. What a gift!

Whenever you feel that your place of worship is too far to get to, do not worry. Just give a loving hug to a child or make a crying child smile and yes, that makes for your prayer for the day! The simple things in life are what touch our hearts. But these are the things we miss out in our daily lives.

A rich and successful CEO of a company may be in need of just a loving pat on his back by his wife; the wife must be looking just for that one compliment from her husband which says 'thank you dear, for working so hard for the family.'

Happiness is a way of life. It is being in gratitude. It lies in valuing the little gifts of life.

A child surrounded with the latest gadgets may be waiting for a few gentle strokes on the forehead by his mother/father which put him to sleep; an old mother may just be waiting for her son to return from the office and report to her in order get the same feeling when, as a little boy, he used to come to her after school and made her feel important.

Is it so difficult? Not at all, but I fear none of us even give it a thought. Our life becomes mechanical and we get so used to all the good things of our life that we seldom stop to just stand and pay our respects and gratitude to people and things that make our life worth living.

"Christmas is forever, not for just one day, for loving, sharing, giving, are not to put away like bells and lights and tinsel, in some box upon a shelf."
— Norman W Brooks

After achieving all the material gains and success, we still wonder as to what happiness actually is. **Happiness lies in making the other person feel better. It lies in loving and caring for others. It lies in the service of others.** Happiness lies in seeing God in everything and everyone. It lies in understanding the fact that all your work and success is not because of you but because of God who wants your good. It lies in offering your every deed to God.

Happiness also lies in discovering your latent talents that will connect you to the inner core of your being.

It lies in being prayerful throughout the day. Happiness also lies in asking God for help whenever you do not understand what to do. Make God your guide and companion because He will always ferry you towards light, towards happiness.

Love grows by sharing. Spread Love!

I told you earlier in this chapter how God likes to give us a little more of all the good things life has to offer. **A prayerful mind does not look for happiness outside;** happiness resides inside our inner being irrespective of our outside circumstances.

Chapter 19

GOOD HEALTH AND HAPPINESS GO TOGETHER!

In the name of working hard, we miss our lunch, do not find time to exercise, forget to have water in between the many cups of sweet tea & coffee, missing out on proper sleep too. This stands true for nearly all of us. After all, it is a competitive world and we have put in efforts and studied to excel. We have to earn money for enjoying a decent standard of living... Have you ever wondered that such a life style can make you sick?

Good Physical and Mental Health are Important

Good health does not include only good physical health. It also encompasses good mental health along with deposits in your social and emotional banks.

We get busy with our job and find little time for ourselves. We do not listen to our bodies, pay little heed to what makes us happy and *just keep running.* Stop today while you are fine and healthy, otherwise you will be forced to rest as a sick and indisposed person! Slow down a bit and assess your life. You will actually be a happy and satisfied person bringing joy in the lives of all those who come in contact with you.

"Happiness is nothing more than a good health and a poor memory."
— Albert Schweitzer

Right nutrition, exercise, proper sleep (at least 6 hours), drinking enough water throughout the day, keeping our body clean, having some time just for sitting in silence, reading a page of your favourite book or listening to 3 minutes of your favourite song — all these can work wonders for your life.

It pains me when I stand near the milk shop in the evening and watch young men stop for a chit chat near the shop while enjoying soft drinks, cigarettes and chips. What nutrition did they take in after a full day of hard work in the office?

On the other hand, in our club, I am delighted to find young boys playing badminton, table tennis and snooker. These boys are in the company of sports. They learn discipline along with the need to keep fit for playing their sport well. I really feel that to bring up a child well, one needs to introduce them to any sport of their choice. Sports keeps you away from unwarranted company and other beverages and bad habits which you may pick up from others.

Live Life to the Fullest

There are many bungalows near my house. One of these stands apart from the rest. It is so beautifully decorated that you will just want to stop in front of this house and adore the beauty and love all around it. There are lovely ethnic paintings on the boundary walls, colourful flowers all around the garden and a swing in the centre with a big search light fitted on it. Then, there are some beautiful bird-houses that look fabulous. It shows the *awareness* with which the occupants are living in this house.

When my neighbour stepped into the house, back from hospital after giving birth to healthy twins, her husband had decorated the home entrance with colourful balloons. WOW! There was so much love in the air. What a welcome! Life is composed of such precious moments — little gestures of love which are inestimable.

Health is Your Real Wealth in Life

'If health is lost, everything is lost' — today I really understand the actual meaning of this simple statement. Most people start morning walks when they are diagnosed with diabetes, blood pressure or other ailments. Why wait? The journey of life is yours and YOU have to take charge of it.

Why don't you start today?
Just 2 kilometres of brisk walking can work wonders for your agility, stamina and overall personality. Join yoga classes for exercise and meditation or Zumba dance classes for recreation along with exercise and keep fit. Hit your nearest gymnasium (but practice push-ups and other exercises only under a well-trained instructor.)

Take Care of Mental Health through Spirituality

Spirituality must be your way of life. It teaches you how to live life and stand up tall even in the face of struggles. When my husband was diagnosed with cancer, we had to plan out for the treatment in another city, while taking care of our kids too. It was not easy but we were strong spiritually. We prayed while also going through regular medication and treatment. We also read some wonderful books which elevated our spirits, emboldened us and reiterated our faith in the power of thought to heal our bodies. Along with medicines, it was also meditation, prayer and positive thinking that worked wonders leading to healing and cure.

Good Health — Best Bank Balance of your Life!

What sort of life are you living? Is it a life full of positive energy and good health? Take care of some simple points mentioned below and realign your life to healthy living —

- Have proper sleep, fruits, enough water every two hours (even while at work), coconut water, orange juice, green vegetables and less of tinned food. It is a good idea to become a vegetarian.

- Do not have *paan* (betel leaf) or cigarettes. Leave these at once and be in gratitude for your good health. Even visualizing the scene of a cancer hospital with its long-drawn treatment can make you shudder. Dump these NOW if you have been taking these injurious things.

- Befriend people with professions different than yours so that you get an idea of life and living other than yours.

- Take care of your body by keeping it clean, bathing regularly and wearing good and colourful clothes (keeping in mind the latest fashion trends!) After all, there is more to life than just working for your job the whole day (and even night!).

- Anger and irritation make you look weak and like a 'victim'. Be a victor instead.

- Have a hobby. Give a good 10 minutes to something you love to do — be it singing, painting, sketching, cycling, playing the guitar or learning a new language.

- Never retaliate or get into an argument. Change the topic or leave the scene but don't become a part of negativity. Assert yourself and reiterate your point of view calmly and with confidence but never become a part of a quarrel.

- Be in control always for this keeps you empowered. Learn to manage people rather than getting affected by them.

- Have proper sleep before you set out for next day's work. Good sleep keeps you rested and in a good mood.

- Never gossip. Use your time for better, bigger and productive ideas rather than discussing other people you do not care about. Why give them space in your mind for free? Also, such negative conversations and thoughts deplete your energy.

- The Past is gone. Look forward towards the future. Never crib. Never repent. You can always start afresh on the canvas of your own beautiful life. Get up and start again. I know, you will!

- Say 'no' to people who pull you down, say 'no' to work that is not on your priority list and concentrate on nurturing your own health, happiness, mental well-being and that of your family.

- Hey! How about a short holiday with your family? This is not only rejuvenating but also an educational experience in terms of meeting people, keeping time for trains and planes, confidence boosting and trying out new things. If you are a good learner, it will surely change your attitude for the better... and good attitude means a successful and happy life!

Lifestyle Changes for Health and Happiness

The Head of Department of a really big organization is lying sick with kidney malfunction. Imagine, is it possible for him to concentrate on his office work? No! He has to go for regular dialysis and has to have so many medicines. Another friend of mine has to take insulin injections twice daily. They all have kept a brave front but would it not be better if we learn from them and make a few lifestyle changes for better health.

"The groundwork of all happiness is good health."
— Leigh Hunt

Have water in place of sweetened tea, smile more, thank the Almighty for your life and all good things and people around you. Live life, love life; for a healthy life is really, really beautiful! All your riches cannot bring back your good health. Stay fit, stay healthy!

Don't start from today, start from now!

Chapter 20

LEARN FROM NATURE

Nature opens us up to the joy of giving. Look at the sun, the trees, the colourful rainbow and singing birds — all are so *alive* to the beauty and love in nature. A mother may stay hungry, but will see to it that her child does not sleep hungry.

There is abundance in nature. One seed grows up into a tree to produce hundreds of fruits which in turn can give rise to thousands of new trees! Nature is all about discipline and balance. Everything happens at its stipulated time. The seasons come and go, flowers bloom to make the world colourful and the sun shows up in the morning to light the world and goes back to rest in the evening — all at the scheduled time.

Like the moon and its moonlight and the flower and its fragrance are inseparable, **love and compassion are the basic tenets of each and every human being residing on earth.** We have to look towards nature and realign with our basic nature which is forgiveness, humility and patience. The nature is furious only when we go against it, spoiling and polluting it beyond reasonable limits.

"If the sight of the blue skies fills you with joy, if a blade of grass springing up in the fields has power to

move you, if the simple things of nature have a message that you understand— rejoice, for your soul is alive."

— Eleonora Duse

Nature Introduces You to the Creator

Yes, where there is creation, there must surely be a creator too! Nature demonstrates to us about how tiny we are in this vast universe and yet how powerful it is to take care of each one of us. Every bird gets its grain each day. Our prayers are answered and the light and heat of the sun sustains life on the Earth.

It is such a dynamic world! Where you see birth, there is death too; where you see light, there is also darkness. We have to live life choosing between dualities and still garner our inner power to maintain truth, love and peace.

God is Working on You Too

Life is an amalgamation of good and bad experiences. However, each one of these is given to us with a purpose. It is said that whatever happens to us, is for our own good since it is God working on us. True, it is.

I actually commenced writing seriously only after I discovered about 'Quantum Mind' and what a drastic difference it could make to one's life at times of stress and difficulty. I wanted to convey about this new found miracle to everyone. So, I started writing the manuscript for my first book *Cancer to Cure* which has enlightened so many people across the globe.

Universe is also Within You

'As within, so without.' In the book *As a Man Thinketh*, author James Allen has reiterated that our thoughts shape our life. **If we alter our thoughts for the better, our quality of life will improve too.** You get what you seek. Align yourself with spirituality and you will discover peace. You will also be able to decipher the world that lies within you! You will understand your own self better, what makes you happy and what your actual interests and inclinations in life are. This knowledge will row the boat of your life towards the coast of happiness.

"I love to think of nature as an unlimited broadcasting station, through which God speaks to us every hour, if we will only tune in."
— George Washington Carver

We are all connected. I am not different from you. This makes your suffering my own suffering! This is what compassion is all about. Love teaches us to be kind and patient. It gives us the power to dissolve envy and hatred, remember the good about everyone and hold on to truth.
We have to plant the seeds of love, peace, gratitude and compassion in our hearts. Real peace does not depend on outside circumstances. Aligning with nature is to align with the source of life. **Let us renew our spiritual relationship with nature (God or the Universe) and with ourselves.**

Accept what life brings for you while keeping the belief that nature will restore your good days without fail. **What is beyond your control, outsource it to nature which will guard you and love you more than you can yourself!**

"Do not judge yourself harshly. Without mercy for ourselves we cannot love the world."

— Buddha

We ought to slow down and enjoy our life. See how nature unfolds slowly but surely. Nature inspires us to just keep going with the flow. Be happy like everything in nature is — the birds, the clouds and the stars. Lao Tzu has said, "Nature does not hurry, yet everything is accomplished." Nature does its own thing, its own way. Go out and discover new paths. Nature will always give you company.

Joy and Sorrow: Two Sides of the Same Coin

Nature is ever changing. In the words of Percy B Shelley, "If spring comes, can winter be far behind?" True, joy and sorrow are present in a rhythmic cycle. When one knocks, the other is waiting just round the corner. So, keep your patience and wait for your time which will be unfurled by nature — just for you! According to Ralph Waldo Emerson, "Nature and books belong to the eyes that see them." Well, there is so much to learn from nature, isn't it?

Chapter 21

WHAT SHOULD YOU CARRY WITH YOU?

The beautiful feature about happiness is that it is already inside you! You have it within you. But we are so engrossed in our everyday activities that we remain unaware of our basic nature of always living in happiness.

Becoming More Aware

Live with awareness. Feel and enjoy the little things that life offers you every moment. We walk past without noticing the magnificent sunrise, the lovely flower and playing children. We can even bring more awareness to our work, thereby deriving much satisfaction and happiness.

To be happy all through the day, carry your smile with you, carry each and every beautiful thought in your collection and yes, carry your music with you! Your smile is the best accessory you can wear with your outfit. Leave behind your attitude of judging people all the time.

Keep your enthusiasm, power to appreciate people and their work and gratitude for all the good things in the world. Respect people for their excellence and achievements.

Fatima sang beautifully at a function at her cousin's place. Every one appreciated her for her beautiful rendition of the song. However, on returning home, her cousins were silent. Though she remained unaffected, it would have strengthened the bond of love between the family had they appreciated Fatima for her skill of singing.

I know a family where the daughter-in-law has worked hard for her personal growth. She has learnt to drive the car, completed her B.Ed. course and teaches in a reputed school. However, the family sees her achievement as her way to be more independent. They also interpret her personal growth as her neglecting the house. They could have supported her in her journey towards success for a happy family life. However, the daughter-in-law now lives in another city with her mother after a quarrel in the family and there seems to be no sign of any party relenting or taking steps to bond once again. They are rich, employed, own a big house but are they happy? Well, anyone can guess that!

While on the move, you can stay tuned to music by humming your favourite tunes and songs. There are some songs which have very inspiring lyrics and can energize you in no time! The legendary work done by great singers, composers and stalwarts in this field is so inspiring.
Keep learning! You can always learn a lot from nature and from people around you. Educate yourself, remain curious, keep exploring because life never stops teaching. You never know when you are inspired!

Gita always kept a small diary and a pen with her. She did not want to miss jotting down beautiful lines of poetry that cropped up in her mind — her moments of inspiration. She has composed her favourite poems in the train, on her way to school and while taking a long ride in the car.

My most prized possession as a teenager was my song book which I packed securely before going out-of-station. I had written the lyrics of all the songs I knew in it. The song book was more like a friend and companion, safely moving around with me. True, it was more than just a diary to me! My mother carries a *Shivlinga* (idol of Lord Shiva) every time she goes out-of-station. She feels that it is like a family member and must be carried along. The *Shivlinga* actually reminds her every moment that she is protected, no matter where she goes. It keeps her connected to the Almighty.

Take your sense of discretion with you while venturing out of your home. In case of arguments, stay away from them because no one ever wins in an argument. Arguments are a sure way of energy depletion.
Carry lot of love in your heart. Have compassion for those who are not as lucky and prosperous as you. A disabled old man begs for alms right at the entrance of a famous grocery shop in my city. Customers buy commodities worth thousands of rupees from this shop. However, when it comes to shelling out a rupee for this man, they detest the idea of giving alms to the poor man.

Compassion teaches us to give without reasoning. However, reasoning coaxes us to think, "why must we be forced into doing something? If we give alms now, many more will stand here. Every person is working hard to earn their bread. Why should healthy and young people beg and make it an easy profession?" Who is right? Think for yourself.

There is another woman in the outhouse of a bungalow who feeds street dogs in her locality every afternoon. It is her own way of serving those she can reach out too. A good deed indeed!

We too buy bread every day, especially to feed the birds and pigeons that come outside our dining room window. When you see the beauty of nature in everything around you and feel the presence of God in animate and inanimate things around you, you will never want to walk away without sharing whatever you have with you.

Sunita has a habit of giving the auto driver fruit or any eatable, that she has bought from the market, along with the auto fare. She does not have to call an auto after her shopping is over— the auto drivers enquire from her if she would like to take an auto back home!

Love is helping and sharing without entertaining the thought of getting anything in return.

Rakesh angrily fumed when he saw young ladies asking for alms outside the temple premises. "They have hands and feet to work hard. Why do they ask for alms?" Every visit to the temple left him angry and he never gave them even a coin from his pocket. Why should he, he asked. Well, we all go to the temple to either ask or thank God for what He has given us. God never questions! He only gives — if not now, at an appropriate time later. So, why should you ask? You are but a mortal soul. Just give whenever you can.

"Start by doing what is necessary;
Then do what's possible;
Suddenly you are doing the impossible."
— Francis of Assissi

Give a very small amount, but maintain the flow. Those who ask alms have their own journey to take. They will learn their life lessons at their own pace. You need not resist. Just give your love. It will make you happy and bring abundance in your life.

NO FAILURE IS FINAL

Success comes only after failure. Failure is not a bad word. It is a necessary step to succeed in life. **Failures teach you what not to do and also give you the advantage of reassessing and improving your work. You are ready to present a better version of your work to the world!** We all clap and cheer for victory but do we ever pay heed to the many hours of practice and toil on which the castle of success has been built up?

"There are no secrets to success. It is the result of preparation, hard work and learning from failure."
— Colin Powell

Success comes to those who stop not. **Success belongs to those who know how to take rejection in their stride and still keep going on with the same enthusiasm and passion. Their work is their reward.** Their focus is on good work which they want to offer to their audience. Every minute detail is well taken care of.

Nalini sang on stage for an inter-school music competition. She climbed on to the stage and made some horrible musical errors! Everything about the song went wrong — the pitch, the beats, the presentation. Well, could you call it a song? However, if you thought that this might have been the end of music for her, you are absolutely mistaken. After all the goof up that day, Nalini pursued classical music and completed the course with a distinction! She has, since then, given many, many stage shows and musical recitals on Radio and Television.

"We all have dreams. But in order to make dreams come into reality, it takes an awful lot of determination, dedication, self-discipline and effort."
— Jesse Owens

My husband reminisces his old days in Medical college when he was a student. Everyone had laughed at him when, in a class discussion, he divulged his ambition of doing super specialization from a premier medical institute of India. Within six months, the results were out and he was surely in — walking into the premises of his dream institution!

Your undoubting spirit and staunch resolution can take you towards success. Get up every time you fall. Be your own worst critic and keep improving in your chosen vocation. God keeps working on us and will give us the gift of success and triumph when He feels we are ready to take on the world! There are instances where a girl paints using her toe after she lost her hands to an accident or a lady who dances on artificial legs!

"Let your dreams be bigger than your fears.
Your actions louder than your words,
and your faith stronger than your feelings."
— Anonymous

To become a plant, the seed has to delve deep inside the ground — in darkness. It thrives there, yearning for sunlight and growth and lo! One fine day it turns into a lovely sapling! A few years after, this plant turns into a fruit-laden tree which has the capacity to produce more seeds and thereby saplings and future trees.

You can realize your full potential only after travelling the tunnel of grilling mistakes and failures. **Improvise, improve and add on, for the better — to reach your destination of success.** But never let failure make you believe that you are beaten!

The only failure is when you say, "I give up!"

Also, have the patience to wait for your time! The moon waits for its turn to shine bright at night. Look at the ants which toil day and night to collect their food. Learn from the bee which makes thousands of rounds to the flowers for collecting honey. Admire the birds which build up their nests by collecting one small twig at a time and build up their nests. Each drop in the ocean is collectively responsible for making it the huge ocean that it is!

Keep trying till you succeed. **Real failure lies in not trying at all.** Continue trying in spite of your doubts and failures. Use all the opportunities that come your way, keep cool, work hard, do away with your doubts and never compare yourself with anyone else.

As Thomas Alva Edison had said, "I have not failed— I have just found 10,000 ways that won't work."

"Most great people have attained their greatest success just one step beyond their greatest failure."
— Napolean Hill

Venus Williams, international Lawn Tennis player said, "You have to believe in yourself when no one else does. That's what makes you a winner." Look at failures as challenges. Every stroke of failure actually brings you nearer to your goal, making you worthy of success that you have been waiting for!

Chapter 23

KEEP YOUR FAITH IN GOD

We all have deep faith in God. Our minds are conditioned to think of God in times of difficulty and pray to Him. However, it is my personal experience that when you are in the midst of difficulties, although you keep praying to God, you also get annoyed. You feel helpless and think that you have to solve your problems yourself. It is only you and the problem in sight. Spirituality seems like a farce when people and friends approach you with 'practical solutions.'

When my husband was undergoing one of the chemotherapy medications, one of our friends suggested that we needed to sell our house (which we had bought on loan.) On his laptop, he calculated each penny we could currently afford to pay. For some time, my husband too aligned with his thoughts. However, I stood my ground saying our loan would somehow be paid and we would live in our own house. Having said that, I really shuddered within. It was not as if my faith in God was any less. But, amidst such reasonable and mathematical calculations, how would I prove my spiritual connection? I prayed to God silently and begged Him to think of ways through which we would not have to sell our house. I also prayed to Him to give me right sense and reason for acting in a practical way.

"Is spirituality for real?" I questioned in my mind!

We came back home to our city after the treatment. After a couple of months, my husband's salary increased by four times and he started earning in accordance with his high educational qualifications as per the new rules of the company! We paid our loan within six months (which otherwise had been calculated to take 20 years!) and became the owners of our sweet home.

Yes! faith did change everything. **You cannot explain the power of faith and prayer to everyone. Each person has his own spiritual journey and will be open to learning new ideas when he is ready for it. He has to empty his mind of preconceived notions.**
While encountering a problem, I hold on to this one sentence — *If you have faith as small as a mustard seed, you can say to this mountain, 'Move from here to there', and it will move. Nothing will be impossible for you...*

Faith Makes Way for Solutions

Keep growing your faith through meditation and prayer. Have faith in God and believe that when you are disheartened with difficulties, He takes charge.

"Faith is seeing light with your heart when all your eyes see is darkness."
— Barbara Johnson

Look at the birds — they start singing much before dawn arrives! That is faith. You make your own efforts and leave the rest to God who will row you past through tough and hard times for sure. He will never ever fail you. Keep your faith and shun your worry and fears.

If God gives the solution, why does he give problems at all?

Well, that is your journey to learn patience, acceptance and compassion. Every difficulty will stir you forward in life. You just have to keep your faith, believe in God, keep praying even though you may not understand His plan at that time. Will worry be of any benefit to you? Never! So, don't worry, just pray.

"Faith in God includes faith in His timing."
— Neal A. Maxwell

God is always there with you and there is a reason for every thing happening in your life. Keep your calm and have full faith in the Almighty. When God gives problems, He also gives you shoes to walk on the difficult path. So, leave your problems in His hands.

"When we have nothing left but God, we discover that God is enough."

There are people who have come out of a vegetative state even after a span of twelve years. Theirs are families who have kept faith for such a long time! The sun shines for you every morning and the gravitational pull of the earth is at work always just like you keep breathing without thinking about it. In the same way, God's love is with you in good and bad times. He waits for the right time to approach your problem and save you from further anxiety. **What you need is patience, prayer and faith.**

"At my lowest: God is my hope
At my darkest: God is my light
At my weakest: God is my strength
At my saddest: God is my comforter"

Remember, in the midst of storms and suffering, God is working for your good. During your good times, He is working to make all your dreams come true. Keep your faith in God. **You will receive more than you expect!** Miracles do happen!

Chapter 24

A HAPPY LIFE IS A SUCCESSFUL LIFE

What good will it be for someone to gain the whole world, yet forfeit their soul? True, you may be rich, famous and may be living in a mansion but if you do not enjoy peace of mind and happiness, you are not successful! You must be satisfied on all accounts — your emotional, financial, social and health banks must all be full for you to be a successful person. There are many more ways in which you can lead a happy life. Actually, little things in life make the big difference!

Limit Your Desires

Happiness in life comes from being contented. You must be ambitious, work hard to improve your designation and living conditions but you must keep a watch on *how much is enough*. You do not have to possess everything you like. Don't pluck that beautiful flower you appreciate; give away the clothes you do not use and do not clutter your house with excess of things. You can also get happiness by giving others what you love most. Try this and you will find for yourself.

Contentment is the greatest form of wealth.

By accumulating things all the time, we are left with little time and space to be grateful for what we already possess! It is our thoughts about what we have which make us happy or sad. Do you know that the best prayer you can send to God every day is 'Thank you'!

"Know that the people who are the richest are not those who have the most, but those who need the least."

— Unknown

We visit places of worship to ask for things we require. One day, when you visit your Temple, Church, Gurudwara or Mosque, just thank the Almighty for all that you already have. Your true measure of success lies in how contented you are.

While shopping for T-shirts, Sunaina buys all seven shades of T-shirts when she is unable to decide which one to buy! I myself kept our old clothes iron in the house thinking that I would require it in case the one we are using needed to be repaired. I read somewhere that if you have not used something for six months, you really don't need it. This made me give the extra iron to someone who did not have one and I am so happy about it. When you give, you attract abundance in your life. In case my iron requires to be mended today, I can afford to buy a new one the same day!

Contentment does not mean Lack of Ambition

You must be ambitious but you must know where to draw the line. A lady doctor works part time but keeps cribbing that her career has taken a back seat because she has to look after her children. This is a wrong attitude. Don't make your educational qualification a problem. Keep upgrading your skill and qualifications and you can always go back for full-time job once your children grow up. You can also think of opening your own enterprise. Work with a happy feeling to attract more happiness in your life. We have to find a balance somewhere. Balance your work, family life and spare some time for sports and exercise in your daily routine.

Contentment also encompasses those precious and joyful moments when you enjoy visiting places, hotels, clubs or sit for watching the latest movie enjoying life utilizing the money you earn doing hard work throughout the year. No, this is not waste of time, as some people may believe. Just like you work hard, you also should learn to sit and relax or do something different and enthuse the child in you! You need to find time for that table-tennis game you love to play or the wonderful book you have always wanted to read! Work while you work and play while you play. You will never grow old — at least not in your heart.

Contentment comes from having enough for yourself and you generate happiness from this state of being by sharing your love, things and time with others around you. For being happy, you need to give happiness and appreciation to others... because what you give comes back to you!

Be Systematic

Keep your surroundings neat and clean. Keep your things in their right places. My father always said that you should be able to get your hands on something you need even in the dark! That is being systematic in life. Do every small act with your mind and soul in it and see yourself succeed. Work hard, be determined and bring your own sunshine and positive attitude in all that you set out to do. Do your work with awareness and love and never give excuses for not having done it well. Confucius was so right when he remarked that life is really simple, but we insist on making it complicated.

"You will never change your life until you change something you do daily. The secret of your success is found in your daily routine."
— John C. Maxwell

One of my friends in the college hostel used to get up really late and start attending her classes from the third period onwards! She was sloppy and kept throwing used clothes in one corner of the hostel room. When there were none left in her closet, she used to pick up one dress from the 'cluttered mountain of clothes' and started ironing it just when it was time to leave for some function or a trip to the market. Today, I can only imagine how she must have kept her house as a married woman! Habits die hard after all...

What You Give, Comes Back to You

True joy comes from giving others. You can give in terms of money, meals, things or even time. **You rise by lifting others, you become rich in happiness by giving.** By giving, you make way for receiving too. Give with love and joy in your mind. Giving is like lightening another's path which actually lightens up yours! Giving is a parameter of how much you love someone.

"There are those who give with joy, and that joy is their reward."
— Kahlil Gibran

One of my friend's family was standing in the club premises with us. They had come there to have a good time together. During a discussion, the lady began complaining about her husband saying that he does not lend her the car for driving. I suddenly saw the expressions on her husband's face turn hostile! Quite natural for anyone. Well, people must learn never to criticize their friends or family members in public. Just tell directly what you want to say to them at the apt time — it is so simple! You too will get the same respect and love which you give to others, making your family a very happy family.

Most people keep themselves engaged on their phones or are too busy to attend to their family when they arrive home. Take care that you do not take for granted those individuals you love the most! Don't fret and fume or complain always. There are many women who complain that they are well educated but have sacrificed their career for their family. Education is an ornament in prosperity and a refuge in adversity. Don't make it look like a problem. Look at it as an asset to your personality. You are well-equipped to stand on your feet and earn a living in case of need.

Keep upgrading yourself and when the time comes, you can go back to work. You just have to have patience and maturity to understand your priorities in life. When you miss out on the growing up years of your children, it is your loss, not theirs. No one can educate your children as well as you will do. You can make them physically and emotionally strong by taking good care of them—and this is not waste of time!

My day started today on a negative note with a phone call from a friend. Well, she was low in energy and deviated to criticizing my husband for trivial issues. I did feel bad and thought I would not ring her again. But thinking about her valuable gifts of time, love and help she has always given me, I rang her again in the evening. She was so cordial and her voice showed that she indeed was sad in the morning for some reason. We talked happily with each other about some really interesting topics and I had a smile on my face when I put down the receiver. I felt proud that I tried to understand her state of mind instead of judging her outright. It is never easy always but trust me, I am happy that I gave her another chance!

Have a Passion, a Purpose in Life

Passion for something in life connects you to a higher purpose. It motivates you to work hard and keep improvising and improving.

Eric Thomas has said, "No alarm clock needed. My passion awakes me."

Following your passion makes it easy to do things, keeps you energized to make improvements and yet you are never tired. With passion, you have the capacity to reach your highest potential. So, follow your passion in life to be successful.

Remember that even if you are very good at your skill, you may not always receive appreciation. You may even be wrongly criticized! Well, that is what is the mark of a great person — he is confident about himself and his abilities and is thick skinned. He evaluates himself and keeps learning for improvement. He does listen to criticism but is never bogged down by it.

Judge yourself lovingly and if you find the scope for improvement, work hard and improve! However, keep a vigil of those who always push you down and leave them alone. Keep away from them so that you don't waste your precious time refuting them or trying to impress them or proving your point to them. Let them not occupy any free space in your mind.

Never Procrastinate

Procrastination is a thief of time. True! When my father pestered us to finish doing a chore then and there, we thought he was not 'cool'. However, now I understand what he meant by saying never to procrastinate. 'Just do it' is the key to success. When you keep your ideas waiting, they get lost somewhere. Remember that work will get done only when you do it! *Do it now* — this is the golden rule you must follow in life. Take a decision whether to do or not to do a work. If you have decided once, just finish doing it.

~~Later~~ Now!

I remember a doctor in a hospital in Bangalore who practiced this. Any query you made, he would enquire immediately and answer you! I was impressed when I noticed that he never procrastinated.

Once we told him not to hurry and give the answer to our query when we came again to him the next day. Well, did he listen to us? No! He called the concerned person then and there, jotted down all the details and conveyed to us right then! He behaved like a true leader. Such an attitude made us believe in him and respect him much more.

Never Speak Ill of Anyone

Most of us waste a lot of time giving our view-point about everything. Just start enjoying silence more. Speak only when needed and filter to see whether it is offending for someone or not. **Spend twenty-four hours without complaining and see how much time and energy you save!** Also, if you speak too much, there are chances that you may speak wrong without giving it much thought.

Never expect anything in return for the good that you have done for others. Just do good and forget. Expectation brings sorrow and resentment. You tend to blame others for the situation you are in and become a 'victim'.

If you really observe famous and successful people, you will notice that they tend to achieve from whatever situation they are in. They make the most of the circumstances they are placed in. They never criticize or condemn. They have a good network of supportive people who bring them business and assignments.

"Judge not, and you will not be judged; condemn not, and you will not be condemned; forgive, you will be forgiven"
— Luke 6:37

One senior doctor we knew did not converse for more than three minutes with anyone he met on the way. In between the conversation, he said 'goodbye' and moved on! I found it quite strange but now, as I have matured, I have understood that beyond this amount of time, most of the people you talk to begin complaining or start a negative conversation! Want to experiment? Go ahead...

Do What is Right

When people hold on to one individual for succeeding faster in life, though they may enjoy short-term gains, in the long run, they incur loss. When the individual they are holding on to goes, they too are pushed into oblivion. However, those who stick to hard work do reap benefits, sooner than later.

Have a set of core values you must follow while living your life. It should be your Personal Constitution.

Life becomes easier as taking right decisions too is rendered simpler.

I visited a boutique shop after my marriage and got confused between three best suits I intended to choose from. I tried my best and then I requested the lady proprietor, an acquaintance, to lend me all three for some time. I wanted to take them home and ask my mom which one to buy. However, she said that it was important for me to take a decision — albeit wrong. She warned me that if I was unable to take small decisions, how would I take the big ones? This incident was an eye-opener for me. I selected one of the three suits and reached home. It was a learning experience for me. Today, I can boast of some wonderful decisions I have taken during difficult times as well as during the most enjoyable times, thanks to her!

Run Your Own Race

It is a good habit to learn from others but be careful never to compare with others — be it material wealth or personal achievements. Too much of competitive behaviour is stressful. On the other hand, if you live in co-operation, you will receive help and support from everyone around you. So, just be you!

"A flower does not think of competing with the flower next to it. It just blooms!"
— Zen Shin

Here's a poem my daughter wrote when she was about 13 years old—

Life

Life is a stage
Every day is a book's new page.
The most of life you should make,
Every difficulty, as an opportunity,
you must take.

What you make out of life: gain or loss,
The choice is finally yours.
Always be in the NOW
For everything in life, be in WOW!

Life's a precious gift from God to you,
One good deed every day, you should do.
Perform your duties and your work,
and you shall surely invite Lady Luck.
Stay positive and have loads of fun
Have a cheerful life in the long run!
Be like the trees, and shine like the Sun
Help everyone, expecting nothing in return.

Life is a gift, make the most out of it
Stay happy, healthy, kind and fit
So that your 'play' is remembered
Reminisced as a hit!

— Composed by Sangeet Pandey

Never Compare with Others

Once you set out to achieve something, do it with total devotion, but never bother about who gets the credit for it. Enjoy the journey and fruits of labour rather than delving on the result of your actions or the credit that comes or does not necessarily come on completion of the task in hand.

"You cannot escape the results of your thoughts. Whatever your present environment may be, you will fall, remain or rise with your thoughts, your vision, your ideal. You will become as small as your controlling desire; As great as your dominant aspiration."

— James Allen

You may be happy with your marks but the moment you learn that someone has managed to score better, your mood alters and you feel sad. Never compare. Run your own race. Do your best and accept the fruits of your own labour with grace and gratitude.

You just have to incorporate a few simple steps in your daily life and you are well equipped to be HAPPY! Find happiness in the little things of life. Be awake to the beauty around you. Meet and greet people but stay away from those who put you down and give you negative energy. Remember, as you think, so you become. Start with not complaining for the next 24 hours, start with sending love and gratitude to your near and dear ones, start by appreciating someone genuinely or just start by sharing with others...

Happiness is our very own nature! Do we need a recipe to remain happy? Actually not! But then, we have long forgotten our very intrinsic nature and gradually drifted into sorrow and distress. Go back again and again to revise and follow methods mentioned in this book and increase your happiness in life. This is the only way to make your *Voyage to Happiness* on the vast sea of life a successful one!

Chapter 25

JOURNEY WITHIN, JOURNEY WITHOUT

For a happy life, what you really need to pay attention to are the really little things in life! If need be, get ready to make some changes within for experiencing happiness and abundance without. Program yourself to remain happy in all circumstances. Your faith in yourself and the Almighty will sail you through the toughest tests of life.

Remember, nothing is permanent — not joys, not sorrows. You need to learn to keep smiling always — which means a happy and successful life. A life that makes you feel good and joyful. A life which is peaceful and open to miracles of nature and abundance of the Universe! A life which kindles you to do better, reach out to more people, share your talents and gifts with others around you and enthuses you to keep getting better and better in your chosen field. A life that makes to give back to society in terms of money and knowledge which will stay even after you are gone. So many inventors, artists and scientists have given inputs so that we may life a comfortable life today. We too should strive to contribute in our small way by spreading the warmth of love, brotherhood, kindness and goodness. After all, this world should be a happy and safe place to live in!

There are many small ways which you can incorporate in your everyday routine and bring great amount of happiness in your life —

1. Start your morning with a good and inspiring book. Read a few pages and remain positive all day long.

2. Watch and read more of positive programmes and news.

3. Take a break in between your work. Also, take a holiday sometimes and just chill.

4. Be soul-conscious. It makes you a more compassionate human being.

5. Do things you enjoy most and complete your pending tasks. It will surely make you feel relaxed and proud of yourself on your achievement.

6. Exercise regularly. If you can't find time to take care of your health, you will have to find time for treatment of some ailment!

7. Don't get attached to things and people. Look forward. Hold on to good memories but remember, you have to move forward. Be ready for any positive change in your life.

8. Let go ego and pride. Always remember that whatever you do, you are a medium of God who is expressing His own greatness through you. Remove the 'I' and use more of 'we' instead. Your success in life is proof of the shimmer that the Almighty has showered on you!

9. Love everyone around you. Well, what about those who

despise you, hurt you? Keep away from them, but don't keep thinking about them or about taking revenge. Bless them and let them be.

10. Meditation, prayer and being in silence are antidotes for happiness. They help you to connect with your real being and you discover your hidden talents and aptitude through these remedies. You travel inwards to discover yourself and lead a happy and healthy life.

11. Practice non-violence in speech and action. You can give to others only what you have. So, if you live in abundance and love, you will be sweet in your speech and loving in your actions.

12. For married couples, a good sex life too goes a long way to keep them happy and satisfied.

13. Financial wellness is an essential factor for happiness. It's hard to smile with a big loan to repay in a couple of months! Save money for financial freedom. You will have to upgrade your skills too accordingly and offer to society services that are most needed.

14. Follow the path of contentment. Measure everything in terms of 'need' or 'greed'. Mahatma Gandhi has aptly said, "The earth provides enough to satisfy every man's need but not for every man's greed."

15. Know that life has its share of joys and sorrows. You have to take both in your stride and keep happy. The circumstances will not always be perfect but you can still smile in deep waters keeping the faith that the light will shine in your life. You have to keep patience and undoubting faith in God.

16. A happy family has some special yet very simple factors like faith, enthusiasm, hobbies, respect, freedom, gratitude, never complaining or fixing blame, and love. They share with each other, care for each other during difficult times and love each other as they are (acceptance) and not as they want the other to be!

17. Acceptance — When you enjoy the good things in life, you never stop to figure out 'why me?' Similarly, at times of distress, keep your patience and faith. Stay on for a while and you will find happiness waiting just round the corner!

18. Have a good sense of humour — Learn to laugh off your follies and those of others. Don't take life too seriously. Be kind to others and yourself. Don't always try to catch people doing the wrong things. Once in a while, just try to spread happiness around you and laugh off your troubles!

19. Sleep well — Before going off to sleep thank God for all the nice things that happened all through the day. Align with nature and sleep by 11 O'clock at night and get up early, around 5 O'clock. Eat well and drink lots of water for enjoying good digestion.

20. God provides — Believe in miracles that keep happening around you at all times!

I was sad that my mobile phone stopped charging and so I had to deposit it in the service centre for repair. As a result, we missed the call from the dentist for extraction of my daughter's teeth scheduled for that month. After a month, when we reached the clinic, the doctor was surprised to find that both her teeth had naturally aligned due to the braces and their extraction was not required at all! I told you, miracles do happen.

21. Don't dwell upon your troubles — When troubles come, try to stay calm and positive. *No storm blows forever!* Instead of worrying about your problem, try to find ways to handle it and solve it. In case of any health issues, reiterate in your mind that you will be alright. Take treatment for it but supplement it with meditation, mild exercises, walking and positive visualization. Visualize in your mind how you will look and feel when you are perfectly alright. Try this and experience healing!

22. Work hard — Hard work will keep you satisfied and give you a sense of achievement. As James Allen has remarked, 'there is good tonic in toil.'

23. Self-scrutiny — Never try to get your sense of worth by what others think of you. You are your own best judge. Analyse your mistakes and try not to repeat them. When you do well, treat yourself and others, pat yourself on the back, enjoy and delight in the glory of your success!

24. Concentrate on your own work and move forward towards success. Love everyone in spite of their mistakes, despite the differences of opinion.

25. And yes, do call your old parents often for you may be busy with your work but they are always thinking about YOU!

26. Hey, why not go out for shopping? Even if you do not intend to buy anything, just enjoy some window shopping! Take your kids along and get pleasure from

your favourite street food. Even shopping is a therapy for happiness! However, remember that happiness derived from outside pleasures stays with you for a short while. When you make it a point to be happy regardless of your circumstances, you are always happy and smiling.

Don't Keep Happiness Waiting!

Let us not keep happiness waiting for us to discover it. **Happiness is not another destination we are trying to reach. It was with us all through our voyage of life.** It eludes us as we are too busy rushing and reaching to finish our daily work. So, happiness keeps following us, waiting for us to give it attention while we look forward — far ahead into the future and keep tensed. We walk, nay, run past happiness!
What we need to realize is that to hold someone's hand, you need to stop, look around positively and offer your welcoming attention. We need to understand that it is the 'journey of life' which brings happiness. Such joy stays with you every moment, every day, bringing more awareness in living, more beauty in life, more wonders in life which further open the treasure chest to miracles, love, abundance, peace, prosperity and happiness.

Tune in to happiness and make it your constant companion. Manage people and situations, learn new and better ways of leading your life, be around happy individuals and create happy spaces where ever you stand. Your *Voyage to Happiness* has made you discover your own self! **What you have altered is only *choosing* to be happy at all times.**

There will be sunshine and thunder, the waves of the ocean of life will be peaceful and sometimes turbulent, you may experience inner upheavals or physical pain — but one thought that will hold you all along in happiness is that *you are the master of your own destiny.*

It is YOU who can *choose* to be happy.

Show your love to people around you. Tell them how much you love them by your small loving gestures like handing them a glass of water, making them comfortable by giving them an extra cushion while they are sitting, helping them, showing acts of kindness, giving thoughtful gifts no matter how big or small — like a special rose bouquet for those who you know love flowers! It can be a cake, a good book, a dish you prepared... anything. Your gift must reflect how well you know the person.

Happiness or Wholeness

Some people condone happiness saying that it counters 'wholeness' in life. However, when we talk of happiness, it is not about winning, receiving, loving and enjoying at *all* times.

True happiness means to be happy even when you are standing amidst adverse circumstances — when you see sickness, sorrow, defeat and failure in life.

True happiness does not depend on outside forces. It means to keep happy, to keep your faith and wait patiently for the tide in your life to subside and normalize. A happy person denotes strength, perseverance, faith and holds on to himself and to the Almighty when things go wrong in life. **Yet, such a person can smile in the storm knowing that the shore is somewhere near. He will adjust the sails, slow down his ship, adjust the compass, change the direction but he *will* keep moving... that's for sure!** A brave heart! Yes, that is the happiness we are talking about here.

"All the world is full of suffering. It is also full of overcoming."
— Helen Keller

Recipe for Happiness and Wholeness in Life

Lead a quality life and make it amazing! Take a flower of sorrow, one of sickness, one of defeat and one flower of pain. Hold them all together to make a bouquet of life. Sprinkle some love, a little faith in yourself, few droplets of patience, faith in the Almighty, be grateful for all the colours of life and your life itself and see how the bouquet shines — fresh and happy!

"The basic thing is that everyone wants happiness, no one wants suffering. And happiness mainly comes from our own attitude, rather than from external factors. If your own mental attitude is correct, even if you remain in a hostile atmosphere, you feel happy."
— Dalai Lama

Live your life fully in the present moment, clear your mind, fuel your soul, change yourself for the better... and adjust your sails. Hey, Captain! Let happiness be your preferred course and your heart become the compass. Actually, your **Voyage to Happiness** really begins *Now*!

Bon Voyage!

ABOUT THE AUTHOR

Sanchita Pandey is the author of six books, of which *Voyage to Happiness* is the second. She writes on health, healing and ways to lead a happy and fulfilling life. Since the publication of her first book *Cancer to Cure* in 2016, she has inspired readers all around the world.

The author also inspires people with spiritual insights and motivational videos through her YouTube channel, ***Inner Universe Community***. Apart from being a writer, she is also a trained vocalist and a very passionate singer, a talent she showcases in her second YouTube channel, **SiNGER SANCHiTA**, which has already amassed thousands of subscribers.

Sanchita has had an interesting childhood, growing up in different parts of India. After graduating with a degree in English (Honours) from Miranda House (Delhi University), she pursued a course in LL.B. (Bachelor of Law) and Masters in Human Rights. Her love for learning further led her to take up a course in M.Sc.(IT) (Masters in Science and Information Technology)

She believes in "feeling good every moment for a happy and peaceful life."

For more details, visit the website:
https://inner-universe.wixsite.com/sanchitapandey

Instagram: @singersanchita
                @inneruniversecommunity

Email: bookings.sanchita@gmail.com

www.ingramcontent.com/pod-product-compliance
Lightning Source LLC
Chambersburg PA
CBHW071425150726
48000CB00001B/485